MISSION
MADAGASCAR

Brian Rawlings

Mission Madagascar

Second Edition.

First published 1997.
This version published October 2021.

Book art+design by Phil Rawlings.
Typesetting main font: Merriweather Light $\frac{(10pt)}{(17pt)}$

ISBN 978-9937-0-9759-8 (hardback colour)
ISBN 978-9937-0-9758-1 (paperback b&w)
ISBN 978-9937-0-9757-4 (ebook)

phoolish
PUBLISHING

www.philrawlings.com

Proceeds from the sale of this book will be donated to the ongoing work in Mandritsara.

Dedicated to the people of Madagascar,
and in loving memory of Sheila.

CONTENTS

PREFACE
Revised 2021 Edition

It is 25 years since my late wife Sheila and I visited Madagascar and I wrote my daily journal. As I stated in the original introduction, it was not intended for public consumption, but was just for personal use. However, I was persuaded to turn it into a book, and its publication was very much a family affair. Sheila typed up my scribblings, I proof read the copy, and my son Phil both designed the cover and arranged for the printing and assembling as a ring-bound paperback book. We had an initial run of 60 copies, hoping to sell these to church members and friends with the proceeds going to the work of HVM (Hopitaly Vaovao Mahafaly) in Mandritsara. In the end, I think we produced and sold around 200 copies, and I was later told that a copy was given to each new missionary arriving at the hospital to give them an insight into the culture and life of the Malagasy people.

Phil is now an author of children's books in his own right, as well as having himself become a missionary working in Nepal from 2011 until 2020, and he thought that it would be fitting in this 25th Anniversary year to produce a new version of the book – as an e-book; a softback and a hardback. I agreed somewhat reluctantly, but it gave me the opportunity to correct a number of typos and grammatical errors that had been missed first time around because of the speed of production. So the main body of text is largely untouched apart from the additions of a few explanations to help a wider audience's understanding.

As well as adding this Preface and Chapter Numbers and Titles to the revised edition, I have also added *Chapter One - The Call*, to give the background as to why and how we came to travel so far for such a short time; and *Chapter Thirteen – An Update: 1997 to 2021*, giving some idea of my involvement in the work since and the thriving gospel and health work that continues there to this day.

I have also added new images scattered throughout to help aid in the story telling. These are in colour in the hardback version, and black and white in the softback. Sadly, due to size limitations they are not included in the e-book.

I have very much enjoyed re-living the experiences and memories as I have revised the account, and hope it gives you as much encouragement, laughter and enjoyment as it has given to me.

Brian, 2021

INTRODUCTION

My original intention was to make brief notes each day as a personal reminder of all that happened and of any amusing incidents during our brief stay in Madagascar at the end of 1996. Once I started, however, it was easier just to let the words flow and tell the stories as they happened, and it quickly became a daily journal. I kept thinking that soon I would be able to stop, because there would be nothing new or different to write about. Some hope! Every day was different, often full of funny goings-on (ha-ha and peculiar), a few of which I have left out to protect other people's feelings.

Each day Sheila would look forward to reading the instalment, and I knew our hosts were itching to find out what I had written, especially when they realised there was a chance of publication to a wider audience.

If you are one of the "stars" of the journal, please do not take offence at anything I have said. It has been done in love and with great gratitude for the life-changing experiences we both had in our short time on the magical island of Madagascar.

Please don't be too critical if some of my facts are wrong – much is my impression of what I have seen and heard. I sincerely hope you will enjoy it as much as I have had and that all readers will be better informed about life on the mission field, as seen by an outsider.

Brian, 1997

CHAPTER ONE
The Call

The story really begins a few years before our visit to Madagascar, when Sheila was employed by the Africa Evangelical Fellowship (AEF) as the telephonist/receptionist at their International Office, which had recently been relocated from London to Newbury. The missionaries in the office had all previously served on the mission field in various African countries and attended and became members of different churches in the town. The Personnel Director, Dorothy Haile, attended Newbury Baptist Church, where Sheila and I were in membership. In 1993, she was asked to give a talk on AEF, and spoke about some land that had just been purchased by AEF on behalf of the Bible Baptist Association of Madagascar, and launched a *"buy a brick"* campaign to raise funds for the building work.

As she was speaking and showing slides of Mandritsara, I heard a distinct message from God – *"one day, you will be going there"*! This was not something that normally happened to me, so you can imagine my surprise, but the call was so clear and unequivocal that I had no doubts that it would happen. I didn't know why I would be going, or how or when, but I knew that one day I would stand in that place.

Our church took on board the need for funds, and raised money for the "buy a brick" campaign, which was asking for the cost of 5,000 "bricks" at £25 each, giving a total of £125,000 for Phase 1, consisting of a basic out-patient medical centre, laboratory, X-ray and small operating theatre. Whilst waiting for these facilities, AEF had hired a building adjacent to the bumpy grass airstrip in the centre of Mandritsara, which was used as a clinic. Building of Phase 1 began in 1993 and was opened in May 1996. Newbury Baptist Church also raised funds for solar panels for the roof of Phase 1, to help with the frequent power outages experienced. Unfortunately, I don't have a record of how much was raised prior to us going, but I do know what we raised after we went (*see Chapter Thirteen*).

After my "call", I shared this with my minister, Rev Grenville Overton, and Dorothy Haile. We then worked towards enabling this to be achieved, which took until October 1996, some three years later. As I am a Chartered Civil Engineer, it was decided that I would be of most use when Phase 2 was due to begin, so that I could help with all the initial setting out and construction work for the foundations. I had to meet and be vetted by AEF's staff (not those that I knew in the International Office!), including Dr David Mann, who was joint Director of the work in Mandristara. I also had to negotiate the time off work with my employer, Sir Robert McAlpine & Sons. I caught my Area Director on a good day, and he agreed to me taking two week's holiday for one year and three week's holiday from the next year's allowance, to enable me to spend five weeks in total in Madagascar. He also agreed to donate the survey instruments necessary – a theodolite and tripod; a quickset level with tripod and staff; and have them air-freighted to Madagascar.

Sheila, of course, working for AEF, had no problems in getting the time off. We had to find the funds to get us to Madagascar, our accommodation in Antananarivo (Tana), and all our food, but NBC very kindly offered to pay for the MAF charter flights between Tana and Mandritsara. So, in mid-October 1996, our adventure could begin.

CHAPTER TWO
Preparations and Departure

Saturday 19th October 1996

We hope to get most things packed, but run out of time. John and Pauline Freeman (the AEF Deputy International Director and his wife) call in to wish us *"bon voyage"* and give us a card. We have had quite a number of good wishes over the last few days.

In the afternoon, David and Jane Mann (AEF Field Director in Mandritsara and his wife, and currently at home on furlough) pop in with their children Rachel and Reuben on their return to Tooting from Bath, having collected them for half term. It is helpful to have some more last-minute instructions, and they give us some letters and presents to take out to their friends in Mandritsara. We also have to find room for some medical supplies, including two X-ray plates, for the hospital.

We relax at the Elcot Park Leisure Centre in the evening, enjoying a swim, sauna and jacuzzi.

～ • ～

Sunday 20th October 1996

All week I have felt a little queasy from the Chloroquine anti-malarial tablets we have to take. This morning's 11.00am service at Newbury Baptist Church includes our valediction, but unfortunately our Minister, Grenville Overton, is away on holiday. Dorothy Haile (AEF's Personnel Director, based in Newbury) gives the children's address, comparing the verse *"Believe in the Lord*

Jesus Christ and you will be saved" in English, French and Malagasy, the language we will encounter in Madagascar. She then says prayers for us as we depart.

We host twenty-two people for lunch, mainly those from AEF who are not abroad at the moment. Late afternoon, I can begin to pack, and manage to complete everything except the hand luggage. The problem is, I can hardly lift the cases because of all the food and supplies Sheila insists on taking! It's a good job we have got extra luggage allowance.

Once again, we decide to relax in the swimming pool and sauna to round off the day.

～ • ～

Monday 21st October 1996: Departure Day!

The morning is taken up with haircuts, packing the final bits and the hand luggage, and a quick swim and sauna at the Elcot – the last bit of luxury for five weeks, but I'm sure there will be times when it feels as though we're back in the sauna! We have lunch with Sheila's mum, then pack up the car ready for the off.

Avon Joyce (a friend at Newbury Baptist Church) has kindly offered to drive us to the airport, and we plan to leave my car at their house so that the engine can be turned over once a week. Our daughter Rachel accompanies us to Heathrow, but son Philip is unable to come because he has to attend a special awards ceremony for the graphics industry – their company has been nominated for an award for his work!

After painlessly booking in at the airport, we have a coffee before saying our goodbyes and making our way to the departure lounge.

The flight to Paris is by Air France Airbus A320, and we have plenty of room as our reserved seats are by the emergency exit door. The flight is uneventful and we are served a snack of rolls and coffee. Arriving at Charles de Gaulle Airport, we transfer by bus from Terminal 2B to 2A and meet Johan Coutigny, the Belgian AEF missionary who is to accompany us. He is normally based in Mandritsara, but has taken time away from his family to assist us. Fortunately, we only have about half an hour to wait before boarding the Air France 747/200 jumbo jet. Once again, Key Travel have done us proud, our seats are 8H and 8J – upstairs, with better legroom and service.

Everything seems to be going to plan, we leave on time – approximately 11.45pm Paris time (10.45pm British time).

~ • ~

Day 1: Tuesday 22nd October 1996

One of the worst things about air travel is that you are served meals at strange times of the day or night. At midnight British time we are offered beef stew with prunes, or hake. I choose the fish, which is not too bad. Sheila decides to do without, because she never travels well. Although we have sufficient leg room, it is not a very comfortable night – the seats give you a numb bum after a while.

I start to watch the in-flight film *"Secrets & Lies"*, but after half an hour the sound goes. I lip read for ten minutes, but decide it is too much effort, so give up and try to snooze. I am amazed that I can still follow the plot, even without the sound.

The African man in the window seat next to Sheila does not speak English or French and is unwell during the flight. He is wrapped in his coat and a blanket but is intermittently cold and hot, yet still manages to sleep most of the way. The other small excitement is when the lady across the aisle from me gets a nose bleed in the early morning which she has problems staunching.

We fly at 550 mph, 37,000 feet, most of the way from Paris to Nairobi, a distance of 5,500 km. Dawn breaks at 4.30am British time, and shortly afterwards we are served a meagre breakfast before landing in Nairobi at 6.30am (8.30 local time). Kenya looks very brown and sparse, with long grass and scrubland. As we taxi towards the terminal buildings, we pass an elegant British Airways Concorde waiting on the tarmac.

After refuelling and taking on board fresh food, we take off at 8.00am for the final almost 3 hour, 2,300 km flight to Antananarivo, the capital of Madagascar, commonly shortened to *"Tana"*. It is uneventful apart from passing close to Mount Kilimanjaro, looking magnificent yet slightly incongruous with its snow-capped peaks in the African heat.

As we approach the west coast of Madagascar, it is hard to put my feelings into words. It seems such a long time since it first became a possibility, now the reality is before us. There is a great sense of anticipation tempered with the slight disquiet of the unknown. My first impressions of Madagascar from the air are of a very barren, hilly land with red earth and vast uninhabited areas. The only habitation we can see are small villages.

We land at Antananarivo (Tana) airport at 12.45pm local time, having left our home almost exactly 24 hours previously. Walking across the tarmac towards the terminal building, I pause to take a photograph of the airport and am immediately stopped by a policeman with a gun. Within two minutes of setting foot in Madagascar, I am almost arrested! Fortunately, we are unable to communicate properly, I plead I am an ignorant Englishman who knows no better and cannot understand what he is saying, and he allows me to continue on my way.

In spite of our previous comments and jokes about "Mad Air", we realise that the jumbo plane that had brought us is Air Madagascar! We later discover that the plane belongs to Air Madagascar, is serviced by Air France in Paris, and is used twice a week by Air France and twice a week by Air Mad.

There is a long, slow queue to clear immigration/passport control, but when we reach the official he is very quick, and doesn't say a word. This is just as well, as we would not have understood him, and would have had to call Johan back to interpret. There is an even longer wait for our luggage, and we begin to think that perhaps it hadn't been put on the flight on transferring at Paris. There are hundreds of people surrounding the small baggage reclaim conveyor belts and no room to move whilst we try to keep our eyes on our hand luggage. Sheila is taken pity on by a porter, who brings a trolley and we load it high with our and Johan's cases.

As we approach customs, Johan is greeted by the young Malagasy mechanic from Mission Aviation Fellowship (MAF) who has come to meet us and help us through. We are asked by the customs officer (through Johan) if we have a video camera or computer with us – things we could sell. Fortunately he doesn't ask Johan directly, because he is bringing in a laptop for Olivier, the hospital administrator. It is also fortunate that he asks us to open the smallest case, which we packed for Tana, because it saves us from trying to explain all the food and provisions we have brought with us.

Outside we are met by Margaret Kundig, the wife of MAF's chief pilot in Madagascar, and Johan deals with the five porters who each lay their claim to a tip for helping us with the luggage. They are not happy with the amount he has given them, and he has quite a haggle until they depart satisfied.

Margaret has come in a battered van, and on the way out of the airport the rear doors burst open without us realising until the car driver behind frantically toots his horn as we go up a hill, worried that the luggage will descend on him! As we later learn to our cost, all of MAF's vehicles are pretty run down, and need to be bump-started each morning. We can only hope that their 'planes are serviced a little better than their cars!

We endure an hours' frenetic drive to Emil and Margaret's house containing the MAF office. The driving style of the Malagasy is suicidal, and there are far more vehicles on the roads than I expected – Tana is a little like the London rush hour without the discipline, lane markings or traffic controls – it's everyone for themselves. Also, the cars are mainly extremely old and battered. Some are broken down in the middle of the road and are left exactly where they came to rest. We pass one such, with broken front suspension, one wheel leaning over at a strange angle.

Emil and Margaret are Swiss and have only recently moved to their house, which is large and airy with a good view. They make us feel welcome and introduce us to the rest of the MAF team, including Mike Frith, the other MAF pilot, who is English. We take the opportunity of sending an email to AEF International Office via David Mann, to let everyone know we have arrived safely.

Tana is very spread out, being located along two valleys separated and surrounded by hills, and the roads do not cross the valleys. This means that driving anywhere is very circuitous, up and down hills and round sharp bends. With oncoming traffic spending a lot of time on the wrong side, it is surprising that there are not more accidents. We are told that people drive after about a month of quarter-hour lessons, followed by a two minute driving test – totally insufficient for hill starts and all the normal driving problems. We are also amazed at the masses of people milling around or by the roadside or at stalls, the majority without footwear of any description. It really is a bustling metropolis.

After refreshment, we are driven to the guest house where we will spend the next few nights. As most of the houses in Tana, it is surrounded by high walls with large metal gates for security. The car sounds its horn and the gates are opened by the maid. The guest house is owned and run by Madame Vao, with help from her two nieces. The guest house is a separate two-storey building to the main house, and we are shown to the Ground Floor accommodation. Upstairs has the better facilities, but it is already occupied by two South African missionary ladies with their three children.

As we eat the meal that has been prepared for us, we hear the family upstairs singing choruses, and we feel serenaded. Our first Malagasy food is tuna steaks in a courgette sauce on a bed of rice, followed by chocolate mousse. We soon find we are very well fed by Chou Chou, Vao's niece who does all the cooking.

The accommodation is sparse but more than adequate. We have a double bedroom with access into a shower room shared with the room next door, which is a single bedroom (for Johan), also containing a dining area. Next to this room is the kitchen area and a toilet. There is no real protection from the mosquitoes, but the windows are shuttered at night. This has the additional advantage of shutting out the light of the dawn, which begins at 5.00am, so that we can sleep on after our long journey.

We finally went to bed at 8.45pm local time, feeling absolutely shattered, having been up for 40 hours, with just catnapping on the plane! We both slept well until 7.00am the next morning.

Madame Vao

Madame Vao's Guest House

CHAPTER THREE
First Impressions

Day 2: Wednesday 23rd October 1996

We enjoy breakfast at 7.50am with Madame Vao in her dining room. Delicious fresh baguettes with home-made jams; strawberry, pineapple or honey – all very sweet. Malagasy coffee is very strong but not bitter, quite enjoyable.

As we are finishing breakfast, we hear the banging of a drum and the blowing of whistles, gradually getting closer. We go outside to investigate and discover it is *"propaganda"* – a group of six to eight men parading and campaigning for the Presidential elections on November 3rd. We ask permission, and they are happy for us to take their photo, both posing and, as they continue on their way, making as much noise as they can.

'Propaganda' campaigning for the November 3rd Presidential elections

Johan needs to interview a possible candidate for the position of building supervisor or maintenance supervisor, and asks me to help to find out the applicant's knowledge of the practical aspects of building. This takes place in the garden in the hot sun. The man is in his mid-thirties and has been recommended by the Pastor of the local Baptist Church. It is very difficult to discover what he knows when it all has to be done through an interpreter, in a mixture of English, French and Malagasy. I am surprised by how much of their conversation in French I am able to follow, although I am not confident enough to speak French myself.

After the interview, we walk up the street from the guest house and at the junction manage to hail a taxi to take us to the offices of MSAADA. They are the Architectural practice responsible for the design and supervision of the hospital buildings. I am introduced to Loren the American architect who is in charge of MSAADA's office in Madagascar. We have a very useful meeting, discussing the progress made on the drawings for Phase 2, the methods of construction, setting out, levels, and so on. We will need to collect the steel moulds that they had made to enable us to construct concrete louvre blocks, required for the autoclave building. We are informed that the drawings will be ready before we depart for Mandritsara, and make arrangements to collect them and the moulds in a couple of days.

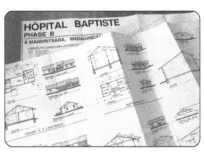

Meeting with the architect   *Drawings for phase 2*

We return by taxi to the guest house to an excellent lunch of roast beef (slightly spiced); carrots and boiled potatoes, followed by banana fritters. Vao takes us to one of her relative's house to try to hire a car and driver for tomorrow. Her nephew is not there, so she leaves a message for him to contact us on his return. Wherever we go, we appear to be the centre of attention, particularly amongst children. Some of the children even beg from us.

We then take another taxi into the city centre to change some of our sterling into local currency. The bank is packed with people of all descriptions, but fortunately the foreign exchange is not busy. We feel a little exposed, however, as we are in full view as we collect our money. We come out millionaires, as we have been given 2.6 million *fmg* (Malagasy francs) in notes. It is a very thick wad that will not fit into a pocket or wallet, so Sheila carries it in her shoulder bag while I try to protect her and the money by walking just behind.

Around the corner from the bank we find a shop selling postcards and airmail envelopes to send home. The stamps we buy are extremely colourful and cost 850 *fmg* (14p) each for airmail. This is cheap compared to the cost of the cards themselves, from 1,500 *fmg* upwards. From this shop we walk up several flights of stone steps to the higher part of the town. All the way along each side of the steps are stalls selling all manner of goods, many of them home-made or recycled. At the top we find a café and stop for welcome soft drinks and a rest. On the other side of the square to the café is a small supermarket. We decide to look around the shop to price up food ready for our main shopping tomorrow. We have to take fresh food to Mandritsara with us, as it will be unavailable there.

From the centre of town we visit an art and craft shop further out of town, and see what is on offer before we visit the market on Friday. This should enable us to barter and not pay over the odds for our purchases. Almost everything can be bartered for here, even the taxis. On our return we are originally asked for 10,000 *fmg*, but haggle the price down to 6,000 *fmg*, which is just under £1 for a 15 minute taxi ride!

Tonight's dinner starts with vegetable soup and is followed by cauliflower and potato in a cheese sauce on a base of mince. Dessert is fresh pineapple. Soon after our meal, we retire to bed, exhausted by a day full of activity.

～ • ～

Day 3: Thursday 24th October 1996

We are woken at 5.30am by Emil when he calls to collect two suitcases. Helimission, the Swiss mission similar to MAF but who fly helicopters rather than 'planes, are due to fly to Mandritsara on their way to pick up someone in the north. In the end it doesn't fly, so the suitcases are left in MAF's hangar at the airport ready for our flight.

When we get up we find the car and driver has already turned up. Madame Vao's nephew, Andry Ranoarimanana has been hired to drive us. He is a young but safe driver, and the car is in good condition, a rarity here. We agree to pay him 100,000 *fmg* for the whole day (about £16), plus his petrol, which is cheap.

After breakfast we firstly go to MAF's office to check out the news concerning my survey instruments, which were due to have been air freighted by my employer, Sir Robert McAlpine Ltd., and also to find out if Margaret is coming shopping with us. Unfortunately, she is too busy today. Johan takes us to the "*Geant Score*" supermarket to buy enough provisions to last the four weeks we are in Mandritsara. At the meat counter, we are served by a tiny young girl who can't even reach the meat at the front of the cabinet. The assistants are all very cheerful and helpful, and understand enough English to get by. We have so much stuff that there is not enough room in the car to take it all with us as well. So Johan returns to the guest house with the boot and back seat piled high, while we wait outside the store for the car to return. We buy ourselves some soft drinks and find some shade to wait in. Just outside the exit a young boy is taken ill. He has a high fever and felt faint, and his mother is worried that he is going to swallow his tongue. Sheila persuades her to remove his pullover, and he still has a shirt and vest on. Eventually staff from the supermarket carry him away to the staff facilities.

We arrive back late for lunch at about 1.30pm, and hungrily eat the chicken legs and rice salad, followed by a fresh fruit salad. Tiana comes from MAF to meet us and is a little late because he has lost the key to his motorcycle and came by taxi. He has the documentation with the Airway Bill Number for the survey instruments, so we all go to the Airport to try to collect them from customs. The officials say they have the packages, but because they are incorrectly addressed they were not able to locate them before. In fact, the address on the instruments is correct, but on the documents it omits the Post Box number!

We have to rush to get to the Airport to try to get them released before the office closes at 4pm. We arrive there at 3.20 and start the ball rolling. To begin, we get the first authorisation from the front desk, then we are sent upstairs for more paperwork, but cannot find the right person for some time. Then we are sent downstairs again to get the boxes out of the pound. However, they need to inspect the goods and do not believe the value of £50 stated by Sir Robert McAlpine Ltd, who have kindly donated them and had them air freighted across. A lot of haggling takes place by Johan and Tiana, who is used to dealing with the officials. Eventually the value is assessed at £100, which means that duty of 290,000 *fmg* (almost £50) has to be paid.

When we hear this, Sheila and I exchange a meaningful look. On my last day at work before I left, someone unexpectedly and generously donated £50 for the trip, saying *"I am sure that something unexpected, that you haven't budgeted for, will occur. This is to help you out."* What a marvellous God we serve, who meets our every need. He knew well in advance of the exact amount that would be required.

Johan and Tiana go off to pay the money, while Sheila and I remain with the instruments, but are beginning to get concerned because the 4pm deadline has passed. Eventually they return with the required receipt and can present the papers to the customs for clearance. At 4.30pm we load everything into the car, relieved that it is all over. Andry drives around the back of the airport to the MAF hangar and we leave the instruments ready for tomorrow's flight.

Survey instruments

Pastor Andrianavalone and his wife

From MAF's hangar, we drop Tiana off in the centre of town, then go to MSAADA's office to collect the completed drawings and a steel mould to make concrete blocks for the autoclave building. Johan has managed to renegotiate their fee down from 7.5% for the drawings and 2.5% for supervision to 8.5% overall, because little supervision will be required for the second phase.

Then Johan has to visit Pastor Andrianavalona, President of the Baptist Union of Madagascar. They ask us into their house behind the Bible Baptist Church, and we briefly meet him and his wife. He speaks a little English, and has visited England.

Andry needs to fill the car with petrol, and the town is the busiest we have seen it, it is clearly their rush-hour. There are long queues of cars everywhere, it is worse than London traffic jams. There are hordes of people on the streets, and lots of food stalls open, selling people their evening meal, even though it is dark after 6pm. Policemen stand on point duty at road junctions, gesticulating and waving frantically, and whistling their directions to each car.

We do not get back to Madame Vao's until after 7pm, and find our meal already waiting for us. We start with cream of carrot soup; then enjoy roast fillet of pork with pasta and a sauce; and finish off with mango and pineapple. Chou Chou is getting better at tea making. Her first efforts were lukewarm, because it was made in the cup with a tea bag, so the water was not boiling. Sheila shows them that it should be made in the pot, but we only got one tea bag in a huge pot. Tonight, however, there are two bags, but it is still very weak. But we're not complaining, we are really grateful for all they are doing for us.

We hear that the plane cannot now take us to Mandritsara until Saturday morning because of MAF's busy schedule. At the moment, Emil is having to fly ballot boxes for the Presidential election to all the remote areas of the country, and in particular to the east, where there are no accessible roads. The small plane is available and could take us, but it does not have enough weight allowance for three people. and all our cases, shopping and equipment. Obviously we have eaten too much here in Tana!! Johan also receives a phone call from Pastor Andrianavalona inviting us all for lunch tomorrow, which he accepts on our behalf.

⌒ • ⌒

Day 4: Friday 25th October 1996

Today is *"Zuma"* (*"Friday"*), the big market – it is reputed to be the biggest outdoor market in the world. We wake to the sound of drums and musical instruments, but we do not know whether this is because of the market or more electioneering.

We have arranged to hire Andry and his car for the morning again. Johan is meeting one of the hospital Phase 1 sub-contractors at 8.15am. He supplied all the doors and windows and wants the release of his retention money. Unfortunately he did not do the remedial work that was required, and Johan had to pay someone else to do it. Today's meeting is to negotiate how much retention money to release to him.

At 9.00am we leave for the Zuma, and are dropped at the bank to change more sterling into local currency, so that we have spending money for gifts. The main market area has stalls which are incredibly tightly packed together, and covers a huge area, so large that we cannot see the end. Each stall has a white umbrella and there are tiny gangways between each stall, making it very difficult to walk with the throng of people.

Similar stalls tend to be grouped together, such as flowers; fruit and veg; shoes; crafts; etc. Once you show the slightest interest, you are given no peace until you make a purchase, then the pressure from other sellers increases when they realise you are prepared to buy something. If one stall holder does not have the colour or shape or size you want, they race off to get alternatives from somewhere else, and find you even when you have walked on.

We first buy some marble eggs. We ask for a pink onyx egg, which they need to bring from elsewhere. While we wait for that to arrive, we haggle the price for both the pink onyx and a blue laterite-stone egg. After we buy these two, we are followed for half an hour by a young lad with a very large pink egg who is desperate to sell it. He keeps coming down in price gradually, starting above 50,000 *fmg* until finally we take pity on him and give him 26,000 *fmg* (under £4).

We then see and purchase some pretty cards made from rice leaves, showing Malagasy work scenes. Sheila shows some interest in hand-embroidered tablecloths, but the first ones we are offered are much too expensive. We are asked 150,000 *fmg* each, but eventually settle on two for 150,000 *fmg* (£24). Then comes the problem, which two do we select? By this time, a crowd has gathered, all with different, large hand-embroidered white tablecloths. After some time, we choose two and go into a nearby shop to get our money out. We are continually conscious of the need to be extremely careful with money. There are large numbers of beggars around, asking, pleading, cajoling for money. They include very young children with small babies in their arms. This is the pitiful side of Madagascar, and it is so difficult to be hard-hearted and try to ignore them.

Pink onyx eggs from Zuma   *Bread basket from Zuma*

The other surprising feature is how well many of the stall holders understand English, especially the younger ones. They know enough to negotiate and help translate for the older ones, so that they don't miss a sale. Another feature is their cheerfulness and ready smiles. When they greet you in French and you respond in English, they reply in English.

After the market, we climb the many steep steps leading to the higher part of town and have soft drinks in the shade of a large tree in an outdoor café. Andry was parked nearby, and Johan joins us in the café before we all leave at around 11.45. Johan decides to go to visit Clint Atkins, an American missionary in Tana who has (literally) thousands of videos that his wife Cathy has all logged and loans out to other missionaries. Beatrice had radioed Emil to tell Johan to collect some more for their use at Mandritsara. Sheila expresses her concern that we will be interrupting their lunch, but Johan assures her that it would be alright. True enough, we arrive as they are just about to eat some pasta, and really spoil it for them. Nevertheless, they make us very welcome, and eventually Johan selects five or six videos, including *"Groundhog Day"* and *"The Money Pit"*.

From their window, we can see a typical scene of women washing their families' clothes in a lake, and spreading them all over the ground to dry.

From here, we still have quite a way to travel before we arrive slightly late at Pastor Andrianavalona's house, where we are expected for lunch. His house (the manse) is built behind the Baptist Church, which is the main one in Tana. The sign is in Malagasy, and its translation reads: *"Church Baptist Bible"*. We learn that the pastor's father was the first Malagasy Baptist Minister in Madagascar, and built the church in 1930.

They have three children; the eldest son, who is 23, was badly injured in a road accident seven years ago and unfortunately suffered some brain damage, and has only been able to start studying again this year. We are also introduced to their two daughters, aged 21 and 15. They have taken a lot of trouble over the lunch. We start with flan and grated carrots; the main course is beef and brown rice, with green beans and potatoes; then there is salad, and cake to finish. It is really too much for us at lunch time, but is very tasty.

Sheila has a very embarrassing experience, which is a repeat of what happened on our previous visit. As we go to the table, Sheila manages to knock over a display. It is made of timber, a stand having a bowl on the top supporting a marble egg. The bowl and all its contents (mainly empty sweet papers!) are strewn all over the floor. It wouldn't have been so bad if she hadn't done exactly the same thing as we were leaving after our first visit there. They must think that she is extremely clumsy!

Their cat keeps making a terrible noise, just like a baby crying. Apparently she has just had two kittens but one had died, and this is her reaction. After lunch, Johan discusses the European Community Contract for the hospital funding with them as they have some concerns with the wording. As we depart, we take photos of them and the church. Very kindly, the pastor offers to return us to Madame Vao's, where we arrive by 3.45pm. We enjoy some coffee, and go for a short walk in the neighbourhood, taking some more photos of local scenes.

On the way back we see an extensive bush fire in the heart of the city, with lots of smoke. Apparently, they often destroy the vegetation by burning, which then gets out of control. This destroys the ground and creates dust bowls – the slash and burn policy that is so prevalent in many third world countries.

~ • ~

CHAPTER FOUR
To Mandritsara

Day 5: Saturday 26th October 1996

The big day has arrived – we are due to fly up to Mandritsara. The Kundigs will collect us from Madame Vao's at 7.45am to take us to the airport. The whole Kundig family will be going with us, staying at Mandritsara for lunch then spending the weekend with a Swiss Catholic nun stationed between Mandritsara and Tana. We settle up our bill. For a total of four nights stay with all meals, we are charged 204,000 *fmg* – just £33! Excellent value, the charge is 15,000 *fmg* per person for bed and breakfast, and 7,000 *fmg* for each meal.

After breakfast, we get our bags and all the supplies ready to load into the Kundig's VW van. The day has started very cloudy, which is disappointing because of photos we want of the flight, etc. However, the day does improve and the clouds break up. The temperature in Tana has probably been in the mid-80's but has felt very comfortable, and the evenings cool enough for Sheila to need a cardigan.

The Kundigs ring at 8.10am to say they are just about to leave their home, which is about a 20 minute drive away. The first problem when they arrive is getting all our luggage, vegetables, groceries, etc. on board with all the Kundigs' luggage. There are the three of us, Emil and Margaret, Laura (their au pair), the three Kundig children who are between 8 and 15 years old and a friend of the middle son, ten people in total. We eventually manage to leave Vao's at 8.45am.

We get to the airport approximately one hour later. On the drive we see many people out and about: one man dressed in a bow tie and white dinner jacket – looking most incongruous amongst people in comparative rags, and he is barefoot! Apparently he would be going to a wedding, and this time of the year is very popular for weddings (like Spring at home).

We see many men removing their bricks from the brick kilns at the side of the roads. The kilns are smoking away and obviously very hot, yet they are standing on the piles of bricks and handling the hot bricks. Alongside the road are many different piles of bricks and lots of kilns. They cut the bricks from the clay ground, mould them into shape, fire them and cure them, all close to each other.

Another busy job that people can be seen doing from the road on the outskirts of Tana is tending rice in the paddy fields. In some places, the earth is turned over and left in large clumps so that it will get broken down by the water. The paddy fields are divided up into small rectangular plots similar to allotments, with high dykes around each plot. The plots get flooded with water, and seeds planted out in seed beds. When the plants reach a certain height, they are pricked out to the right distance apart. They tend the plants until they need to be pricked out. They will not survive if too dry, but drown if too wet; the crops can be ruined in the rainy season. Oxen are used to plough over the ground before planting.

We arrive at the airport to discover that the MAF mechanic is busy washing down the aircraft: a ten-seater Italian twin turboprop, with navigational aids – capable of instrument landings. Everything has to be weighed on the scales, including each person, hand luggage, main luggage, food, etc. Emil realises there is not enough room for all the luggage, so he removes two of the seats and places a child between each adult. So the seating plan is two in the front (including the pilot), then three, three and three (each set of three people occupying only two seats). Even then we are very hard pressed to get everything in, but while we are still trying to shoehorn it all in the space behind the last two seats, Emil finishes the task of adding up all the weight and discovers that we are 60kg over the limit. He offers to stop Margaret from going, but that is not acceptable. We decide to reduce our luggage and provisions by 60kg and send it to Mandritsara by truck. This leaves each Friday, arriving in Mandritsara on Sunday. Johan has a case that is almost completely full of his children's clothes that obviously aren't required yet, and he also leaves behind a tent that was for use when they travel to the villages to carry out inoculations and evangelism. Unfortunately, his case was the first thing we had loaded on the plane, so we almost have to remove everything else first! Then we unpack the food supplies, removing all the tinned food, some potatoes and other non-perishable goods, until we manage to reach 60kg. Then everything has to be repacked in the back of the plane, covered with netting and strapped in.

MAF flight, Tana to Mandritsara   *Rice paddy fields in Tana*

At last we are ready to board. We arrived at the airport at about 9.40, and we climb aboard the plane at about 10.15 for the preflight checks. Everyone is strapped in, the children with special child lap-belts. Sheila passes around the mint imperials.

I sit next to Emil (on his right), with Sheila behind me and Johan next to her and Tobias between them. To balance the weight, Emil positions us – either me or Johan had to sit beside him (being the heaviest), and Johan allowed me since it was my first time and so that I can take photos. The plane is jump-started using a large set of batteries to save the plane's batteries. All the necessary checks are done, we taxi to the holding area and the engines are run up to full speed.

Then we ask permission from Air Traffic Control to take off. Our call sign is Tango Papa. All radio contact with Air Traffic Control on this flight is carried out in French. The aircraft needs about 360m to take off. It is very smooth, there is a short bank to left and then a smooth climb to 13,000 feet, which takes 15-20 minutes, up through the clouds. Sheila is okay at this stage, and both of us are taking pictures.

Emil keeps up a constant commentary about what he is doing, intermittently reporting to ATC. He makes adjustments to the computer database, which is programmed with every airport or airstrip in the world, and should be updated monthly. There is no need for this in Madagascar, because the things that could change (the approaches, for example) do not change and it is costly. When it is programmed from airport A to airstrip B, it gives a read-out of the distance, course (true and adjusted for wind direction), estimated time of arrival, the airport's height above sea level, etc. Mandritsara is 1,040 ft above sea level (320m), and Tana is 1,500 ft above sea level.

We do not pass over any towns during the flight. Most of the area is mountainous, very dry and barren, mainly coloured brown or red with some areas of green forest. Miles and miles of deserted highlands, with little or no population.

As we approach Mandritsara, we could see that the town nestles in a bowl, surrounded by hills on all sides. In the hills and further beyond we can see occasional villages – groups of 20 or 30 huts – which form part of the area served by the Hopitaly Vaovao Mahafaly (HVM), which means "Good News Hospital" – literally "the hospital *that brings good news"*. The nearer we approach Mandritsara, so our excitement mounts. Emil needs to fly around to check the wind direction for landing, so he does a circuit over the airstrip and gives us a chance to see the hospital from the air – situated on the edge of town, about two Kilometres from the centre. The aircraft performs a tight bank, and this causes Sheila to lose her stomach. Another tight bank, and then we come in to land, and we can see hordes of children racing from all over town as they hear the aircraft approach. We also make out the reception committee at the airstrip, surrounded by young children. We come in fast due to the excessive load, and on touch down Emil puts on the nosewheel brakes for a short distance then releases the brake, before finally braking again until we reduce to taxiing speed. This is necessary due to a bump a third of the way along the grass "runway", which on a previous landing had broken the nosewheel. Now Emil is aware of it, he carries out the above procedure. We turn and taxi down the strip to the waiting crowds and two Land Rovers. It is quite a reception! Annie (the laboratory technician) and Beatrice (head nurse) soon step forward as I get out first, followed by Emil who positions the aircraft steps for everyone else to disembark. They are closely followed by Dr Adrien (joint hospital director with Dr David Mann) and Olivier (hospital administrator) who enthusiastically shake our hands and welcome us to Mandritsara.

Annie in her laboratory

Beatrice in the courtyard

•

We load up the Land Rovers and drive the short distance to the compound. The main house stands alongside the road, one of the few tarmac roads in Mandritsara. Behind the main house are containers and out-houses, all surrounded by a timber fence. The compound stands alone, with nothing around it. Dr Adrien lives a short distance away.

The Kundigs come back with us to the house for lunch which the girls had prepared that morning. We only have time to briefly get introduced to Idoxy, a Christian girl who does the gardening and will buy meat for us from the market (very early in the morning to get the best cuts – a fillet steak of beef is 16,000 *fmg* for 2 Kg = 60p/lb!!). We place our luggage in David and Jane Manns' part of the house where we will be staying in their absence on furlough and unpack the vegetables and frozen meat we bought in Tana. We discover that not all of the meat had been frozen at Madame Vao's and had only been in the fridge – we hope it has survived the flight and nearly 4 hours out of the fridge!!

One thing that hit us as we got off the plane is the heat – it is much hotter in Mandritsara than Tana, over 90°F. As the afternoon wears on, however, a breeze gets up and makes it much more comfortable, particularly in the evening. There is a full moon, making it very beautiful on our first night there.

Lunch is spaghetti bolognaise followed by fresh fruit salad and banana ice cream (just made). After lunch, we return to the airstrip with the Kundigs to see them depart and take pictures of the plane taking off, he then did a fly-past for us.

We return to the house and I unpack our cases while Sheila sorts out the food and kitchen. We are surprised to see that the main door into the Mann's part of the house is through the bedroom, although there are patio doors into the living room around the other side of the house. We unsuccessfully search for adaptors for the electrical sockets, although David Mann had told us there were plenty around! It is a good job we brought two adaptors with us. We also look for a torch in case of power cuts, but only found them the next day and we needed to charge up the batteries.

Adrien and Gisele (Adrien's wife, who is in charge of the Good News School) bring their children, Numan, Nathaniel and Nehemiah, to see us and welcome us during the afternoon. Later we are invited to supper upstairs with the girls, on the flat roof area outside their rooms. It is very pleasant up there (but much too hot during the day). We enjoy soup and rolls, followed by a salad of salami, egg, cheese, green salad and bread, then bananas to finish with. To end the day, we watch a video film *"The Money Pit"*, a comedy which we all enjoy. Then we can retire to bed!! A long and tiring day, but with all the excitement it is not a particularly good night's sleep.

～ • ～

Day 6: Sunday 27th October 1996

I arise at 6.45am, shower and breakfast on cornflakes (Kelloggs bought in Tana) and toast with home-made marmalade (Sheila's Mum's).

Church is supposed to begin at 8.30am so we all leave the house at 8.20, even though it is a seven to ten minute walk. The church meets in a building by the airstrip. The service cannot begin until Sunday School ends, so it often starts late. Today it starts at 8.45, and finishes at about 11, with the communion service afterwards (but we do not stop for that).

The Service is led by Pastor Julien, with Dr Adrien preaching. There is a time of praise, a prayer, the children's address, the reading, sermon, then the notices, all interspersed with hymns, and they end after further singing. The Notices section takes longer than the sermon, because reports are given by all those who have been away – on holiday, on evangelism to the villages, news of deaths or other information, etc, etc. Visitors are warmly welcomed – we are asked to come out to the front and bring greetings, and the Pastor invites me to preach at a future service.

There is a creche for children aged 5-6 years and below, who leave after the children's talk and we can hear them singing to tunes we know. Almost 50 children go out into creche, and more than that number remain throughout the whole service, for over two hours! There are probably 80 to 100 adults, and all the seats are taken, with many of the children sat on the floor. The seats are wooden benches, some with backrests and others without, but none are very comfortable after two hours!

The choir sing three pieces during the service. All the singing is very tuneful, and we borrow a Malagasy hymn book from Beatrice to follow the words as best we can. Johan helps me to follow the sermon, based on Romans 15 and 16. He speaks about the differing gifts of the people listed and the importance of all working together as a team, and compares this with the work of Medecin Sans Frontier. The service is about to end when a helicopter is heard arriving, so all the children are in a terrific hurry to get out and greet the helicopter, which is bringing one of the candidates in the election for a political meeting.

They have a terrific way of ensuring that everyone shakes everyone else's hand, which apparently is common in many African countries. The first person out stands by the door, and each subsequent person forms a queue behind the Pastor (or the first person out). As each person exits, so they go down the line shaking everyone's hand already in the queue and then joins the end of the line. This means that we repeat the greeting "salaama tompko", and shake hands about two hundred times!

After this ceremony, the members go back inside for communion, which lasts about 20 minutes, and their church meeting follows. Beatrice, Sheila and I return home instead. Lunch is a barbecue upstairs with the girls and Johan. We barbecue sausages and kebabbed beef – which is very tough. We hope that it's not all like that. With the meat we have baked potatoes, potato salad and lettuce. This is followed by Belgian chocolates (pralines) from Johan, and coffee. Sheila feels brave and invites everyone back to supper in our temporary home.

The afternoon is spent leisurely. I look everywhere for adaptors again, unsuccessfully. However, I find some torches and start to recharge batteries for them, which I leave on all evening. Sheila and I visit Gisele to see when she will be able to accompany Sheila to the market, and they arrange to go on Tuesday at 8am. Gisele and Adrien live in a white house a very short distance away.

Beatrice arranges with Idoxy for her to go to the market first thing tomorrow morning (6am) to buy us 2 kg of beef fillet, some onions and bananas. We give her 25,000 *fmg* (£4), and she came back with 3 kg of beef! (about 6.5 lb).

Gemma, the Manns' black and white cat, is starting to come into the house. She makes such a fuss, sitting outside the mosquito screen with the living room door open, crying and mewing for attention, that it is easier to let her in for a short time. She does not seem to be fed quite enough from Idoxy, so we give her the occasional titbit, milk, or cold tea.

For supper Sheila prepares pumpkin soup to which she adds a chicken oxo, an ordinary oxo and an Indian oxo: it is quite spicy but nice. She cooks some bread (from a packet mix for quickness) to go with it and makes it into a plaited loaf and some small rolls. The plaited loaf is delicious, and Beatrice is delighted because it is shaped like a traditional Swiss loaf. Soup is followed by cheese on toast with tomatoes and cucumber. Our guests leave at about 8pm and we play Tri-Ominoes for a short time after I write yesterday's journal. By 10pm we retire to bed and have a good sleep.

CHAPTER FIVE
Getting to Work!

Day 7: Monday 28th October 1996

We are suddenly woken at 5.30am by the distressing sounds of wailing and crying – apparently someone had died in the Government hospital just down the road from us. I get up at 6.15am ready for a 7.30 start. Johan is not quite ready, so we do not leave until almost 8. We drive to the hospital in Johan's Toyota pick-up, and it seems quite a long way along the dry, dusty, and bumpy road. It is okay in some parts but others are badly rutted, which slows the journey down. The French roads contractor, Colas, has apparently recently repaired the road, but after the rainy season it will be very bad again.

The schools are on holiday, so there are lots of children around. As we pass, lots of them excitedly shout *"Salut Vazaha"* – *"hello white foreigner"*, and wave, and love it when I wave and shout *"salut"* in return. About three quarters of the way to the hospital is a large three-storey house painted in garish colours – pink, yellow and blue – which looks most incongruous amongst the red-brown hills and drab huts all around. The ground floor is a shop, and the building has been erected by a man who supplies medicine and drugs from Tana and does very well from the business, as there is no competition.

At last I can see beyond a small village the white water tower of the Hospital, and we swing round to enter the open gates set into a high brick wall. At the left hand side of the gate on the wall is a large signboard, showing the opening times and other details in Malagasy. The people don't yet bother to read it, and turn up whenever they feel like it.

The morning evangelism and healthcare talks are just finishing, and we see quite a number of patients waiting in the open area of the out-patients department as we pass and park in the maintenance service area. Johan's maintenance men immediately come over to greet him and also greet me, shaking my hand politely. This is repeated with everyone I meet. They are very polite and courteous people, with smiling faces and are extremely welcoming.

There is a succession of men to see Johan through the day, asking for work. He already has six men on his staff, and takes on a further six to start tomorrow, and puts others on first reserve for next week, when we have had a chance to assess how many we need. We expect to build the numbers up to 20-25 depending on their productivity.

We start on a tour of the hospital, and Dr Adrien officially welcomes me to HVM. There are three doctors on duty today, and Monday is always busy. I am impressed with the building work generally – the brick and stone is clean externally, all the walls are plastered and painted. The internal joinery, such as cabinets, shelving, cupboards, worktops, etc. are all locally made. Much of the timber has not been seasoned properly and so has warped, but otherwise the joinery is of good quality. Even the towel rails, which fold back, are in timber copied from European design but are an improvement.

In the X-ray department I am greeted by Theophile the X-ray technician and immediately thanked for the X-ray plates I brought out from Dr David Mann. He is delighted with them. It makes carrying these heavy objects worthwhile. The X-ray room has lots of high-tech equipment still waiting to be installed – this is one of Johan's important tasks. It is functioning at the moment with an adequate but old US army field machine.

The operating theatre is unusual by European standards because it has a number of windows on two of the walls – I am told this was a request by David Mann to avoid boredom amongst theatre staff during long operations.

Signpost to the hospital

Phase 1 of the hospital

Waiting area with X-ray plate drying

The Manns home nearing completion

The house being built on the site for the Manns is very good. The main room will have beautiful views both ways of the rolling hills and mountains surrounding Mandritsara. It is very well equipped in terms of size, having a lounge and eating area in the centre; an office, kitchen and utility room to one side of the central area; and three bedrooms and a bathroom on the other side. The only problem appears to be the very narrow doors, which will make bringing furniture in and out very difficult. Along the front of the house is a veranda area, and a small one at the rear outside the utility room. It will be extremely pleasant when it is finished. To be completed, it needs windows and doors fitted;

kitchen units; plumbing and sanitary ware; electrical fittings; and painting.

As it is our first day, Johan needs to see his maid (to make bread dough for him) and I need my calculator, we decide to return home for coffee at about 10.45. Sheila is very surprised to see us! This morning Sheila has prepared the 3 kg of beef Idoxy bought from the market. She froze two pieces for roasting, and has minced about 2 kg, getting blood all over her and the floor with the hand mincer. Some she will use as mince and some as beefburgers. Gemma the cat managed to sneak in and pinch a piece of meat when Sheila turned her back to answer the door.

After coffee Johan and I drive into town to select and buy timber for profiles for the setting out. We select five long pieces of hardwood sized 10cm x 10cm (approximately), which is not very straight, and 5 planks – twice as thick and wide as I need, but all they have. These are also hardwood, softwood is not available. We transport it further down the main street to the timber yard where Johan asks the carpenter to cut each stake into four (approx. 2" x 2"), and each plank into three. I am really going to have fun trying to nail it onto the stakes!

On our return to HVM we decide on the priorities for building – to start clearing shrubs and topsoil ready for the laundry area, and start the foundations for the autoclave room, which is a small extension to the existing out-patient building and is located next to the operating theatre to enable instruments to be sterilised. The room is required because of the high temperatures the equipment generates, which needs to be dissipated, and for safety in case the pressurised equipment explodes. Hence part of the walls of this building needs to be in special "louvred" blocks, and MSAADA have designed and had made a special steel mould for the blocks to be cast with a louvred shape.

We return to the house for lunch at about 12.45 to find that Sheila has cooked us casseroled veal and dumplings, mash potatoes and cabbage; followed by peach flavoured instant whip. As Johan has to bake his bread, we don't get to return to HVM until 2.45, which does not leave long until the hospital closes at 5pm and we return home at around 5.30pm.

Johan appoints one of his men, Jean, as foreman for the works. Two men start to clear the topsoil and vegetation for the laundry area, and I set out the foundation trenches for the autoclave building. The dimensions do not quite match those on the Architects' sketch – the building will be approximately 8 cm short, but this does not appear to be critical. Jean starts to dig trenches, using the marks and pegs I have provided. On checking the Architect's drawings, I find some discrepancies.

We leave the hospital at 5.30, and along the road pick up a large number of hospital workers walking home, including Olivier, so there are six inside and a further eight men in the open pick-up.

When I arrive home, Sheila suggests that we walk to the restaurant to buy some cola. However, it is shut (although Johan said it is open all day), so we decide to try a shop I had seen with a "Coca Cola" sign over the door. They have none, but point to a nearby bar. Then the fun starts, as we try to get them to understand that we want two large bottles of coke and one of orange. As we have only returned two empty bottles, we have to pay extra for one bottle. The price is 4,000 *fmg* x 3 for the drink and 2,000 *fmg* deposit for the bottle: i.e. a total of £2 for the coke and orange plus 30p for the bottle.

On my return home, I take a shower with just hot water (solar heated) because once the cold water tap on the shower is turned on, we find it is almost impossible to turn off. Johan had looked at it at lunch time but could not turn it off at all, but I manage and eventually get the knack of it.

Supper is scrambled eggs and Johan's fresh bread, followed by melon. This is white and quite hard and almost tasteless, very disappointing. After tea I write my journal and manage to get a very good reception for the World Service news at 6.00pm GMT from the CD radio player Annie has lent us. This keeps us in touch with the outside world's news most days.

～ • ～

Day 8: Tuesday 29th October 1996

Sheila is off to the market today with Gisele. Idoxy babysits for Gisele so she did not have to take her children. As they approach the corner of the road to the hospital, an ox and cart tries to turn the corner and the ox nearly knocks Sheila over as it careers towards her at great speed. Most of the stall holders sit beside the road with their little mounds of goods for sale, and make up everything into piles that cost 500 *fmg* (8p). This is so that they don't have to give change – the smallest note is 500 *fmg*.

Hence, you can buy: five tomatoes or five onions for 500 *fmg*; three tins of tomato puree (not fresh but the best they have) or eight cups of rice for 1,500 *fmg*. No bags are provided, you have to take your own.

Gisele buys two eggs, and to test they are fresh, a bowl of dirty water is used. If the eggs float, they are bad. The locals only ever buy enough food to last that day, because they have been brought up without 'fridges. Gisele wants baking powder and goes from stall to stall but cannot find any. Sheila offers her some that she had brought out with her.

Gisele is a Malagasy who has not been abroad and speaks very little English, but is very willing to learn. As they approach the house on the way back, Gisele asks if that was Sheila's washing she could see hanging up. Sheila explains that at home we have a machine to wash the clothes, and one to dry them – this surprises her, until it is explained that you could not always hang the washing outside in England. Then she is told that we even have a machine to wash the cups, plates and saucers – which amazes her, and Sheila can picture her imagining the cups and saucers revolving as in the washing machine.

Today is very hot. The excavation for the autoclave building is complete, so we check the levels and bang pins in the formation to give the top level of the concrete foundations. I start to explain to Johan how to use the level and read the staff – he is very keen to learn for when I am not around.

To check levels, the quickset level is fixed to a tripod and the instrument levelled in two directions at right angles, using a bubble set into the baseplate (like a spirit level). The staff is a telescopic box section 3m long in three pieces, graduated all along its length in millimetres, centimetres and metres by alternately coloured markings. By looking through the level at the staff, the same level can be transferred or different levels established.

We are then ready for concreting. I start to set out the lines for the laundry and wash area trenches, completely on my own – I am becoming quite adept at improvising in the way of working alone. This is not easy, when it is necessary to both look through the theodolite and knock in a peg in the right place!

A theodolite is an optical surveying instrument with a rotating telescope for measuring angles, both horizontally and vertically. It is set up on a tripod, like the level, but is slightly more difficult because it needs to be set up vertically over a known line or setting out point, yet remain horizontal. The line can then be extended, or a line 90° to the original (or any other angle) can be set out. It is also important that the instrument is at the most comfortable height to look through the telescope, again not easy to master at first.

I establish a temporary setting out point which is surrounded with concrete, hopefully so that it will remain in position for further checking. I use the theodolite to turn 90° from the line of the existing wall, which will form the back wall of the laundry. The foundations here will be about 20cm deeper than the autoclave, to match the existing.

The first batch of concrete looks terrible – all stone and little cement. The specified concrete mix is 1:3:6 (cement, sand, aggregate), but I discover that they had used one bag of cement to three wheelbarrows of sand to six wheelbarrows of aggregate, instead of using a gauge box!! Also, the aggregate was 50mm down instead of 25mm. By the fourth and last batch it actually starts to look like concrete. They don't think curing is necessary as the evening would be cool (70+°F), but I put them right by explaining that we cure concrete in England, no matter what the weather, to prevent cracking. They learn very quickly, and are very keen to please.

We discover that one of my slide films has been put into Sheila's camera by mistake, so we have been taking double slides of everything! We have two cameras, and the intention is that I take slides while Sheila takes prints.

Lunch is spaghetti bolognaise followed by banana sponge pudding and custard. Supper is beefburgers and bread rolls (but all home-made!).

We try unsuccessfully to send two emails, one to Philip, and the other to AEF International Office. The good news is that we receive two emails – from Philip and Tim and Carol Kopp, AEF International Director. There was another from Philip the previous day, but no message!?!

～ • ～

Day 9: Wednesday 30th October 1996

We rise at 6am, although there is light from 5.30, and plenty of activity outside from before 5am. As the majority of people have no electricity, they have an early start and early finish to match the hours of daylight. It is also cooler to work in the early morning.

A man comes to the hospital this morning with samples of his bricks, which he had made. They are well fired and fairly consistent in size, but are 10mm too small for correct bonding. He says that there is no problem in increasing his mould size. The requested price starts at 150 *fmg* for each brick but is bartered down to 110 *fmg* each (about 1.5p). He then wants paying for the three brick samples he leaves with us (all of 5p's worth!). He is told that he will be in competition with others for the supply. Johan suggests that he and I should go out into the villages soon to look at brick making and try to find a suitable supplier.

Sheila writes a note to ldoxy using the English/Malagasy phrase book we find on the Manns' bookshelf. In it, she asks her to buy a chicken to cook on Thursday, ready for the picnic on Friday. ldoxy is highly delighted with the note, and roars with laughter. Even though the wording is not quite correct, she understands what is wanted. She will go to the market very early on Thursday morning (probably before we are up), buy and bring back a live chicken, then kill it at home, pluck it and prepare it for cooking. Sheila also asks to take photos of her doing this.

Gisele calls in for coffee and offers to take Sheila to the market again on Thursday. Tuesdays and Thursdays are the main market days.

Lunch today is pork casserole and local rice. The meat is very tender, and is casseroled with onions, aubergines, and courgettes. To follow is toffee-flavoured angel delight.

After lunch I drive the Toyota pick-up the 2 km to the hospital. It is quite an experience avoiding the pigs, dogs, ox carts, small children and large stones and ruts in the road. In the rainy season, the road is often impassable so they have to walk. On the way back from the hospital, we are asked to use the vehicle as a temporary ambulance – a woman has suffered a reaction to an injection and feels very poorly, so we transport her home.

Sheila hears some small boys playing football outside, so goes up onto the roof to take some photos. As soon as they see her they stop playing and pose for the photos instead of being natural. The vast majority of people here love having their picture taken and beam to the camera, but expect a copy of the photo to be sent to them. We will have to order double prints of all our films and send one copy out with David and Jane for them to distribute.

Supper is home-made pizza, which is very tasty.

This evening is the Prayer Meeting in Johan's home. Dr Adrien; Olivier and Ravo; Dr Jeannine; Dr Hanitra; Beatrice; Annie; Johan; Sheila and myself attend, only Gisele is missing from those who normally attend. Annie leads the devotions from the letter of Jude, which Dr Adrien translates for Ravo, because her English is poor (but much better than our French or Malagasy!) Prayers are said in either English or French, which is an interesting experience. Phase 2 features prominently in the prayers. Sheila gives a report on the staff at AEF International Office, especially remembering Tim and Carol Kopp after their recent motorway accident (which we heard on our email last night).

At 9.10pm local time (6.10pm GMT), Carol Winfield rings – what a pleasant surprise! She says that she is really trying the number out for Sheila's mum, who will ring another time, but we have a good chat nevertheless.

~ • ~

Day 10: Thursday 31st October 1996

Today is the day for the live chicken! At about 5.30am we hear Idoxy return from the market with the fowl cackling away. At about 8am she comes over for Sheila to take a picture of the chicken still alive before she kills it and prepares it for the oven. You cannot get fresher meat than that! After this, Sheila visits the market with Gisele, buying five tomatoes for 500 *fmg*; five bananas for 500 *fmg*; some ginger for 500 *fmg* and three garlic bulbs for 500 *fmg*, a grand total of under 35p! They try to get a pawpaw, but there are none available. The melons we have had so far have been tasteless.

Along the way to the market, Sheila sees building workers moving bricks. Instead of using a hod, they throw the bricks up one at a time – very time consuming. As they build, the bricks are laid dry, without any mortar. The walls are then daubed with a clayey mud which dries very hard, and holds the bricks together.

On her return, Idoxy takes Sheila to her house to watch her prepare the chicken. Unfortunately, (or maybe fortunately!) she has already killed it and removed its head. She places it in a bowl, and pours boiling water over it. The feathers can then be easily removed. After this, she removes the giblets, and it only takes about 20 minutes from start to finish. The locals use the head and giblets for a meal. It is a small chicken by our standards, and Sheila boils it in the oven. In the evening it is cut up to take to the picnic tomorrow, with all the pieces used for a chicken and rice meal.

Chicken in baskets

Plucking the chicken

Sheila is feeling a little unwell today – a streaming nose, high temperature, sore throat, and aching. To cap it all, the maid wax polishes the living room floor and she is allergic to the wax – it causes her to sneeze incessantly, and her eyes are puffy and red. She manages to cook for lunchtime but I dish it out and wash up etc, as she is in bed when we arrive back for lunch. We are over an hour late because today the HVM senior staff have their monthly business meeting. They still didn't manage to finish it, so it starts again at 3.30pm and we do not leave the hospital until 6.00pm. By this time, of course, the sun is setting and it is danger time from mosquitoes, so I am wary of being out without adequate protection. Johan is not eating with us this evening, so it doesn't matter quite so much if we are a little late home.

When we return to the Hospital after lunch, the weekly prayer meeting had just started for all the hospital staff. It is well attended, and Dr Adrien leads it. Staff are asked to share, or for any prayer requests. It is very informal and light hearted, the Malagache have a great sense of humour and are continually laughing. It is all conducted in Malagasy, Johan translates some of it for me so that I can follow what is going on. Four or five local staff pray before Dr Adrien stops the prayer session and the notices take place. Of particular importance is the picnic for all staff and families tomorrow, which is All Saints Day, a public holiday.

They also make a presentation of a small gift to the medical student who is due to return to his studies after his three months' practical experience at Mandritsara. He has apparently been very useful around the hospital, helping out wherever needed, including X-ray; pharmacy and administration. He is clearly well liked, and hopes he will be able to return when he qualifies as a doctor.

Lunch is roast fillet of beef, mashed potatoes, carrots, green beans and bubble and squeak. Bananas for dessert. Supper is rolls, using up the remains of the bread, and salad.

Each day the weather is very similar. The early morning is bright and sunny with occasional clouds off the hills. As the morning progresses, the clouds get burnt away and it gets hotter and hotter. In the shade it is usually quite comfortable because there is always a strong breeze, and is sometimes very windy, but in the sun there is no let up. Most days it is well over 90°F (34°C). About 4pm it cools off a little, and the evenings are extremely pleasant outdoors, but can be a little warm and stuffy indoors. The nights are quite warm, but we sleep with a window open (mosquito screened) and the resulting breeze makes it comfortable.

We don't seem to have much problem sleeping, we usually go to bed 9.30 to 10 (which is early for back at home) but we wake quite easily at 6.00am. It has been light for ¾ of an hour by then.

~ • ~

CHAPTER SIX
Public Holiday, Picnic and Election Day

Day 11: Friday 1st November 1996

Today is a public holiday, All Saints Day, so we are able to take advantage and sleep in until 7.30am!! Outside is quiet for a change, not the normal hustle and bustle from 5.30am onwards. Usually we hear the zebu (ox) carts rolling slowly down the road outside taking families or produce to the market, and people up and about in the comparative cool of the morning (mid-70's°F). Even so, it is difficult to sleep on when the light is so bright outside and the sun streams through the bedroom window.

Today the hospital has planned a picnic for all staff and their families, lasting from around 10am to 4pm. It takes place in a delightful mango orchard just off the road to HVM and just outside the main town of Mandritsara. Adjacent to the orchard is a large grassed open area which we use for playing games, but normally accommodates the weekly cattle market. People come from miles away driving their herds of zebu, which are often left under the control of young boys. The grass is sparse and brown, waiting for the coming rains. Apparently the whole area is transformed into a mass of green all over the surrounding hills and mountains in the rainy season. At the moment, everything is dry and parched, at its driest, and covered in layers of red dust which blows everywhere as people, carts, cattle, bikes, etc. churn it up or the wind whips it up into miniature dust storms.

Everyone gathers under the trees for shade, sitting on raffia mats from their homes, in groups and families. The picnic starts with Dr Adrien and Olivier teaching everyone a new chorus written especially for HVM – the team's "theme song". We are accompanied by Theophile, the X-ray technician, who has brought his guitar along. The Malagasy people are very tuneful and not afraid to sing out. The new chorus is very catchy and the tune and some of the Malagache words keep coming back to mind throughout the day – *"Fahly fahly, izao, izao .... Alleluia, allelu"*. I have asked Johan to write down the words in Malagasy and English so that we can recount it later. It is sung as a round, with different people or groups starting and the rest following, and everyone enjoys it.

The hospital staff picnic

After more singing, Adrien brings a brief message from John 15:1–8 concerning Jesus being the vine, and we are the branches, and that we should always abide or rest in Him. He graphically illustrates this by having a small boy break a thin twig in two. He then takes similar twigs and binds them to a branch. It is impossible to break the twig while it is attached to the branch. What a simple illustration that is a good lesson for us all!

There is more singing, then Johan talks about the next phase of the hospital, explaining the buildings to be completed and the sequence, and why it is necessary to do it in three stages. This is related to the draw-down of money from the European

Community, when and if they execute the Contract. Questions are invited, and it is established that Phase 2 will take a total of two years to complete.

All the singing, talking and obligatory notices (mainly advertising a get-together at Christmas) takes about an hour from the start time of 10.15am.

Robust games follow, which the locals enjoy greatly, spending most of the time laughing. The people go into separate groups – most of the men play football, while the children and women play other games. Annie and Dr Jeannine teach a group of very small infants to play boule, which is very interesting to watch.

At 12.30, Annie is hungry and impatient for her lunch. So she honks the horn of the pick-up, a Toyota 4-wheel drive, five-seater vehicle with an open area at the back. It is a signal to Adrien, the football referee, that time is up. He immediately blows his whistle and everyone rushes over to get ready for lunch.

Olivier gives thanks. Each family has brought their own food and drink, although Beatrice has brought two large barrels of water – one for washing and one for drinking. Our lunch is the chicken Sheila cooked yesterday – it is very tough and not as much taste as ones at home, even though it is very fresh – with a slice of ham, two slices of cheese, lettuce and tomatoes, and home-made bread. It is *"serra be"* – very good. This is followed by water melon (bought in Tana) which was excellent, and banana. Johan has brought a lemon drink and coffee. There's nothing quite like a picnic in the open air.

There are three men that I recognise from the permanent staff in the maintenance / building department – Radesina (the storeman); Flavien (the carpenter); and Jean (the foreman). Jean shows his talent at guitar playing – what a refreshing change to have a building foreman who is a committed Christian!

After lunch, everyone except Adrien, Olivier, Johan, Beatrice, Annie, Sheila and myself are divided into four teams. There are over 100 people there. Each team has to undertake one of four specified tasks in rotation. At Olivier's area, the team has to find out answers to specific questions – for example: how many people are there on the picnic? At Johan's area, there is a quiz relating to HVM and the missionaries: e.g. in what order did the AEF missionaries first arrive in Mandritsara? At Beatrice's area (where we are), the team has to pretend that they are journalists and find out as much as possible about Sheila and I as they can in a specified time. The only problem is, all the questions have to be asked in English! This is Adrien's clever way of getting everyone to know more about us, whilst at the same time teaching them some English. Those that cannot speak any English ask Bea in Malagache who then gets them to repeat the question in English. It causes much amusement.

Some of the questions they ask are very good. Most of them ask our names, where we are from, when we came and when we would leave, how many children we have, their names and ages, what we all do, our hobbies, sporting interests, etc. We feel almost ashamed when someone asks how many cars our family has, to answer four, one each. There are probably a total of under ten cars or Land Rover type vehicles in the whole of Mandritsara! They also want to know about our church; how many members it has; if there are a lot of Christians in England (NO); Why not? (because they are hard-hearted towards God). Almost each group wants to know what the weather is like in England now – cold and gales!

The fourth exercise is to write, perform and dance a song based on any verse or verses from John 15:1-8 about the vine and branches. For an impromptu performance, this is extremely well done by all groups. Two groups stand out, however. One forms two lines and does an excellent dance routine whilst singing a very tuneful melody. The group that receives most applause, however, is the group that is led by Jean, the building foreman, on the guitar. Their tune is very catchy, the rest of the group do actions to the words, and they sing well. Both these groups are made to perform again before the winners are announced to great rejoicing and applause. Points scored from each phase are totted up to give an overall winner.

It is now about 3pm, and the effects of her cold and the heat have taken their toll on Sheila, so Annie brings us home and then returns to see the picnic out. We hear them all return soon after 4.30pm, worn out but encouraged by such a worthwhile event. It has been terrific to see the camaraderie and team spirit evident amongst all the hospital staff, a real joy in their relatively simple lives. What a privilege it has been for us to join in such celebrations.

Dr Adrien calls round to see if we would like to join them for a meal tomorrow lunch time, and we say that we will look forward to it. Normally on a Friday or Saturday evening, the girls go out for a meal at the local "Restaurant". Steak and chips is the top item on the menu, but it must be booked in advance to make sure they have the meat. Beatrice had booked for us all to go on Friday evening, thinking it would be good not to have to cook after the exertions of the picnic. In the morning, however, the restaurant had come to say they had not been able to get steaks, so we postpone our evening out until tomorrow. Instead, we dine on lasagne and salad.

Friday night is video night. We all gather in Johan's living room at about 8.15pm after our evening meal, and decide which video to watch. Someone selects *"Revenge of the Pink Panther"* which is a suitable light-hearted way to end the day.

Just before this, we receive a further two emails; one from John Turk sent on 31st October, which we should have received before, and the other from Liz Legg at International Office which includes a message from Sheila's mum. Liz's letter is quite long and chatty and it is clear from the contents that at least some of the emails we have sent have got through. Unfortunately, it is difficult to tell which ones, and from where they were sent.

~ • ~

Day 12: Saturday 2nd November 1996

We again rise at 7.30am and enjoy a leisurely breakfast, before Annie asks us if we want anything from the market, as she's just about to go. We decline as we want to look at it ourselves and take photographs. It had been a hot, sultry night without much breeze, and it stays that way through the day – quite still, close and humid. Johan says he thinks the early rains may be coming – short but heavy bursts of tropical rain – also called the *"mango rains"*, necessary to ripen the mangoes.

We walk down through the main street, past the market and up the hill on the far side, past the main church in the town, the Lutheran church. We are on our way to the post office with postcards put into air mail envelopes and stamped with the extremely colourful stamps for which Madagascar is renown amongst philatelists. The cost is 850 *fmg* (about 9p). Everywhere we go, we are the centre of attention, especially with the children. Many adults offer us courteous greetings, some in French. I see Monsieur Azad, the shopkeeper from whom we bought timber during the week, and he greets me with a cheery *"Bonjour monsieur, comment ca va?"*.

At the top of the hill along the dusty and rutted road by the church, we stop to take photos – back along the main street, of the church, of a beautiful gardenia tree covered in white flowers which has a marvellous scent. Just then a cart pulled by two zebu (ox with a hump on their shoulder) and driven by four young boys (no older than 10!!) passed by and we paused to take their picture.

On to the Post Office, with photos of Sheila posting the letters.

We hope they are received well before we return. We don't know how often the post box is emptied, or how mail gets sorted. What we do know is that mail is returned to Tana each Tuesday on an Air Madagascar flight and can often reach Europe within a week. Over the entrance to the Post Office is the inscription *"Post & Telecommunications Mandritsara"*. Outside is a monument in stone which looks like a map of Madagascar. It stands about 10ft tall, and has the date *"1958"* engraved in it. We will have to find out what it commemorates, and guess it is probably independence from France. We later discover that it celebrates the beginning of independence discussions, which was actually achieved in 1960. The Town Hall is located almost opposite the Post Office.

We descend back down the hill, pausing to take in the views of the town spread below us, and search for the house we are staying in on the hill on the opposite side of town. Two young boys, each carrying a bundle of firewood over their shoulders and one with an axe, pause to have their photo taken, giggling as they carry on their way.

It is time for us to make our purchases, and go past the *"bus station"* where the taxi-brousses line up to transport people into Tana (some two days travel) or into the neighbouring towns. They do not leave at any set time, but wait until they are literally overflowing with people inside and out, and have baggage piled high on top.

Ebu (ox) and cart in Mandritsara   *Market day and taxi brousse*

Outside the market is a terrible stench of rotting fruit and vegetables, just thrown down on the ground, so we quickly enter the open area where each stall holder sits on the ground with their wares spread out on mats in front of them. Their produce is grouped in little piles, each pile representing the amount you can buy for 500 *fmg* (8p). So there are piles of five tomatoes, five onions, etc. We buy ten tomatoes (two piles, but surprisingly still only 500 *fmg* – perhaps they took pity on us); five onions, ten bananas, and three large limes. We try to buy some spring onions but have trouble over the price – we cannot understand how much they want. Since the smallest note is 500 *fmg*, you really need to buy something with the spring onions, since they are only 100 *fmg* each bunch. Sheila will buy some on Tuesday with Gisele.

We look at the meat stall in the covered part of the market and decide it is just as well we do not have to buy our own meat – everywhere is covered in flies and there are dogs searching for scraps on the floor. There are no hygiene precautions at all. Sheila even has the gall to take some photos – I'm not sure if they will come out, because it is very dark in there.

Outside the meat market and to one side, are piles of dried fish, different types and sizes, all looking and smelling most unappetising except to the masses of flies congregating around the fish. There are even so called "fresh" fish just allowed to lay in the hot sun with an occasional flick of water to make them look fresher. Sheila won't even buy any for the cat! There are also some live crabs which are splattered with mud to keep them alive and from drying out in the baking sun. With Mandritsara being so far from the coast, it is very difficult to have fresh fish available.

We are beginning to feel the heat and humidity and decide to buy a bottle of Fanta when we buy the litre of Coke we also need. As we walk along another road lined with stalls which display their wares on the pavement outside, we stop to watch a young girl of about two. She is oblivious to everything around her, and is carefully washing her feet and legs. She has a small bucket of water beside her; first she applies some soap then pours water from the bucket over her feet and legs. Her father sees us watching his daughter and laughs as he realises what she is doing and calls the girl's mother to see. Several other onlookers join in the laughter, the girl still caught up in her own world.

Sheila tries to take a photo of an old woman she had previously bought from, who jabbers away in Malagasy without stopping, but she hides and refuses to come out. We buy the litre of coke, and pay for the bottle, plus a small bottle of Fanta orange to drink immediately and head back home. The stalls nearer home are now selling hot food, things like Yorkshire puddings, rice cakes, journey cakes, etc – all fried in the open. We trudge back up the hill towards home, grateful for the cool of the interior of the house. We can now have a rest before we prepare to go to lunch at Dr Adrien and Gisele's – *"Papa and Mama Numan"*.

Sheila buying onions and limes   *Girl washing herself*

As we are about to leave the house, Adrien comes for some cold filtered water for us to drink at the table – his house does not have a water filter. Johan was supposed to let them have some, but was delayed at the hospital unloading a container. He arrives shortly after us. As we arrive, the whole family line up to greet us formally to shake hands, including the two boys, Numan and Nathaniel. Nehemiah, the baby, is sleeping in another room.

Our meal has already been prepared, and we are shown to the table. There are chicken pieces, marinated and then cooked in a garlic and onion sauce; pieces of beef with greens similar to spinach, cooked in delicately flavoured spices, and, of course, rice. No dish in a Malagache household is complete without rice. They have a saying that your hunger can never be satisfied unless you eat rice. The Malagache use spices a great deal, but none of them are strongly flavoured. Even the garlic and onions are very mild.

For dessert we are served a banana and pawpaw fresh fruit salad. We express surprise, because we have looked for pawpaw in the market but could not find any. Gisele says that she bought from someone at the door. The dessert is excellent, very refreshing after the pleasant meal.

Dr Adrien, Gisele and children

Homemade bread

Adrien has spent many years abroad, in France and Zaire, and has visited many other countries including England, where he studied for a short time. He even visited AEF in Newbury when the work in Madagascar was being planned. He speaks Malagasy, French, and very good English. When I preach, he will translate into Malagasy. He is an excellent leader and motivator, a good preacher and is co-director with David Mann of HVM. He also plays the piano and guitar, and writes songs!! What a gifted man, with a real compassion for people and is a lovely gentle man. It is a privilege to know him.

After coffee, we depart. It is traditional not to linger after the meal. Back at the house it is time to bake bread from scratch, and we want to try to bake a decent size loaf as we would buy back home. Sheila has brought a recipe book with her on bread-making, and we religiously follow the instructions using dried yeast, and making enough for a 2lb loaf tin. One of the problems is the time it takes – between each stage the dough must be left to rise by placing it in a plastic bag in a warm place (no problem here, everywhere is warm!). It seems to work very well. After all the processes, the dough is flattened out into a rectangle, rolled like a Swiss roll, the ends are tucked in, and it is dropped into the loaf tin. It is again left to rise, then baked in the oven. The smell of freshly baking bread is so mouth-watering, filling the house with the heady aroma of yeast. We set the alarm for 30 minutes, but get impatient after about 25 minutes, anxious to see our first efforts.

What a delight when we open the oven door to see the loaf perfectly formed, and looking like real bread. We have to take photos, and do the rounds to Johan, Beatrice and Annie to show it off. Olivier and Jeannine are also in the house, and admire our efforts. Now Sheila won't be so bothered to try again.

In the evening we are off to the Restaurant for our pre-ordered meal of steak and chips. Bea is feeling very hungry and orders a Chinese soup to start. We had a large lunch so are content to just eat the main course. The steak and chips come, but they would not be recognised as proper steaks at home. The chips are excellent, because of the oil in which they are cooked. It is local oil, made from peanuts, and can be bought in the market. The others tell us they will take us to see it being made. In fact, we don't find time to go to the village where they make it. We return to the house by torchlight, and the others join us for dessert: strawberry or chocolate angel delight.

At about 9.45 we decide to ring Philip and Rachel to let them know we are well, and hope preparations are okay for their bonfire party which is shortly to begin. Rachel says Grandma is hoping to ring sometime next week, and that she (Rachel) has received promotion and a pay rise. Philip tells us he sent another email last night but has not received ours! Johan will check the emails tomorrow night.

And so to bed – another day packed with fresh experiences. I keep thinking I will soon run out of things to write about, but it is getting longer and longer and longer!!!

～ • ～

Day 13: Election Day: Sunday 3rd November 1996

As we enjoy a leisurely breakfast at about 7.30am, we hear the urgent sound of a tooting horn. It is the truck arrived from Tana, earlier than expected. It left Tana on Friday, but often doesn't get to Mandritsara until late afternoon on Sunday. The lorry backs into the compound, with its rear near to the store that most of the goods we are expecting will be kept. First off are six drums of aviation fuel for MAF as there is nowhere at the airstrip for them to store fuel, and as they sometimes need a refuelling stop, AEF agree to keep the drums for them. They have two sets of fuel, because the larger MAF plane uses different fuel to the smaller one. They also keep yellow drums for Helimission, and together with AEF's diesel drums, the place is awash with fuel! The arrangement suits AEF though, because apart from helping MAF out and reciprocating for some of the ways they are of assistance to AEF, it means that MAF are more likely to land at Mandritsara.

There are two large boxes – one full of plastic bottles for the hospital, and the other containing the food supplies we had been unable to put on the plane a week earlier. In addition, we had radioed MAF for extra things we could not obtain in Mandritsara – UHT milk (the cows are not producing milk at the moment because the grass is non-existent, waiting for the rains); tomato puree; and strawberry "*sirop*" – a sweet flavoured cordial for diluting with water. The truck also brought Johan's suitcase and tent that had been left in the MAF hangar, and gas bottles for cooking and for the hospital. Bea has been expecting a consignment of Bibles, and is disappointed that it has not arrived. The total charge for the transport was 125,000 *fmg* (£20) for a journey of almost 300 miles and two days. The amazing thing is that there are six men on board who help to unload!

It is time to get ready for Church, and it is clearly going to be a hot day as we walk the ten minutes to the building the Church presently occupies. The wind has dropped and it is muggy, and inside the building it is destined to get even hotter. We are able to enter almost as soon as we arrive, and take our place at the very back on an upright wooden pew that is uncomfortable after ten minutes, let alone another two hours! Worship takes place in a lean-to with a corrugated roof with small holes in it, peppered about randomly. The floor is smooth concrete, brown with the red dust that permeates everything. It is clean and functional, but no fancy finishes, and extremely basic. The doors and frames are rough timber, and the doors into the creche, close to where we are sat, are wet with new paint, spread very thinly over the bare wood beneath.

The room quickly fills, and Dr Adrien stands at the lectern at the front of the Church ready to begin. He leads worship today, with Pastor Julien, a young Malagasy, preaching. After a hymn and prayer, Adrien gets his guitar and proceeds to teach the congregation two songs. The Malagache are very quick to pick up new tunes and words, because of the tradition for handing things down by word of mouth. The second song had been specially selected by Adrien to get us involved. He teaches the verse first in Malagasy, then French, and then English and it is a real joy to hear everyone singing in English (and it means we can at last have a good sing).

The words are :-

"Jesus, Jesus, Lord to me,
Master, Saviour, Prince of peace,
Reign within my heart today,
Jesus, Lord to me".

We have been invited to lunch with Dr Jeannine. She lives in the upstairs part of a house in the centre of town, close to the taxi-brousses collection point, the Air Madagascan office and unfortunately near the electricity generator which makes some noise. When we arrive she is without power. It is just as well that everyone cooks by bottled gas, because electricity is very expensive. Jeannine works at the hospital and is a specialist in anaesthetics, so is keen for the oxygen equipment to be up and running. She spent a number of years in France both training and practising, but has returned to Madagascar to a considerably lower standard of living. Doctors at HVM only earn 600,000 *fmg* (less than £100) per month, and she lives in just two rooms, sharing a shower and toilet with Dr Hanitra, who is an eye surgeon. Jeannine has to cook in her bedroom and her sink is on the veranda. The dedication to return from Europe to such conditions is truly amazing. She speaks French very well, of course, but has not used English for many years. As the lunch progresses, her English improves, and with my little French and Johan to help out with French and Malagasy translation, we have no problem in communicating, Jeannine even asking us about *"mad cow disease"*!

Jeannine has also invited Julia, a young Malagasy agricultural engineer working with the Department of Agriculture to improve rice planting methods and yield in the rural areas, in the villages around Mandritsara. She is fluent in French and Russian, having studied at Kiev before glasnost, when Russia encouraged many African students in the Communist era. In spite of this, Julia is a keen Christian, and we had met her both Sundays at the Baptist Church. She is the first, and up to now, only female Malagasy agricultural engineer, and finds it difficult gaining acceptance in some of the villages. It is very interesting talking to her.

Lunch is once again delicious. In spite of Sheila's prior doubts, she thoroughly enjoys the meal. The starter is green pawpaw, shredded and cooked in oil with a little pepper. To follow is chicken pieces cooked in fresh coconut milk and a delicate mild curry, with rice and chopped tomatoes. Dessert is fruit – mango (green mango cut into pieces, boiled in sugared water for ten minutes and allowed to cool), or fruit known as the *"heart of a cow"* because of its unusual shape. It has fairly large black pips in it (like water melon seeds), and the texture is creamy and not unpleasant to the taste.

During dessert the power comes back on, and a car hoots for Julia. She has to return to the village she is living in, 18 km away (12 miles) to vote. After coffee, we descend the steep stairs into the garden to find that one of the hospital workers is waiting to speak to Johan. His sister is very ill and he had cycled to Dr Adrien's for help. HVM is not open on the weekends, and has no in-patient facility yet, so Adrien suggested that Johan could transport the worker's sister to the Government hospital in his pick-up.

It appears the woman has malaria, and it is imperative that she be treated immediately. After Johan takes her to hospital, Beatrice visits her and discovers that the Government hospital does not have the drugs prescribed for her by the doctors. They are hedging their bets, by suggesting anti-malarial drugs, antibiotics and aspirin! So Bea has to drive to HVM to get the drugs, while Annie takes some blood samples to carry out tests on Monday – it proves negative, but since treatment has already started, this would have affected the result.

We all get together for a barbecue in the evening, up on the roof. It is an interesting exercise, cooking chicken breasts and sausages by torchlight. It is amazing what a difference in temperature there is between downstairs and upstairs. During the day, upstairs gets very hot, but in the evening the cool wind makes it very comfortable. In fact, after a while Sheila gets quite chilly and needs to put a cardigan on! It must still be over 20°C though! It is a very clear night, and the stars are shining brightly, more apparent because of the lack of background light. Very beautiful, and of course the stars appear a little different because we are in the southern hemisphere.

~ • ~

CHAPTER SEVEN
Shoeboxes and Sourcing Materials

Day 14: Monday 4th November 1996

I awake at first light once again, before 5am, to the sound of women pounding rice ready for their meals that day. It is hard work, better done in the cool of the early morning. The cockerel crows, dogs bark, and the early morning sounds of the sleepy town gradually awakening become apparent.

Before we can travel to work, we need to change a front wheel on Johan's Toyota pick-up which has developed a puncture. This does not take too long between the pair of us, and we finish in time for Johan to contact MAF on the radio for their regular daily report – usually around 8am. Today, however, he can only raise Emil, who is in the air. We discover later that Margaret could hear Johan but could not reach him, probably due to atmospheric conditions.

On arrival at the hospital, we find 18 to 20 men waiting for us, looking for work. Johan and Jean (the foreman) select a further eight to go with the 12 we already have, but offer them work on a daily basis to make it more flexible. There are also more groups with samples of their bricks, two of which fail the *"drop test"*. One brick is dropped from a height of about one metre onto the edge of another. If it breaks, it is clearly not strong enough. A very simple but effective test where British Standards and ISO 9001 quality assurance regulations do not exist.

It is important for us to set out the first ward block to enable a start to be made on the excavation of the footings. While Johan deals with the extra labour and brick suppliers, I set up the theodolite. Johan and I just start the setting out, which I explain step by step to teach Johan so that he will be able to carry on by himself on later stages of the project after his return in January, when Annie rushes over to report that the centrifuge is not working properly. It keeps overheating and cutting out. It is an essential tool for the blood samples, and the only other centrifuge at the hospital is already broken, awaiting repair.

Supervising Johan setting out   *Digging the autoclave foundations*

So I continue alone, while Johan tries to repair the centrifuge. One of the brushes is sticking, and breaks as he tries to remove it, so he needs to get a replacement. Out comes the other centrifuge, which has a faulty timer switch that does not allow it to stay on – the ratchet has worn loose. By lunchtime it is re-assembled and ready for use, a great relief to the technicians who can otherwise only prepare one sample at a time by turning a wheel – very laborious and time consuming.

The day has been very overcast and I forget to put any sun cream on. Despite no sun being evident all morning, by midday my arms and legs are quite red and feeling a little sore.

Sheila has a busy morning. Beatrice has given her a list of all the curtain sizes required for each room at the hospital, together with the material and her very small electric sewing machine (with instructions in German). Most of the morning is spent cutting out each curtain length, and there is only just enough material to go round. There are 22 pairs of curtains required!

The rest of the morning Sheila spends addressing and writing all the Christmas cards she bought in Tana. They are not really Christmas cards, because in Madagascar the shops don't begin to sell them until December, but they show typical work scenes from Madagascar, have the name of the country on the front, and have a message in French. The messages are slightly different, to the effect that once you have been to Madagascar, you will want to return; and when you leave, a part of your heart is left behind. These sentiments certainly echo our own feelings. The cards are unusual, but we're sure people will understand the reason we are sending them just this once. (We have heard since that some people want to keep theirs, so are having them framed).

Lunch is a welcome break for both of us – chicken supreme with rice, peas and sweetcorn, followed by banana sponge pudding and custard. Then we hardly have time to sit down before our return to work.

We continue the setting out of the ward block and show Jean what needs to be done. The excavation for the laundry and wash area foundations is complete, but the last part of the digging has taken a long time because the ground is so hard. We place short lengths of reinforcing rods in the excavation to give levels of the top of the concrete footings, and I supervise Johan setting up the quickset level and taking readings on the staff. It won't be long before he is confident enough to do it alone.

In the afternoon, Sheila continues to help the AEF and HVM staff by sorting out all the Christmas gifts sent to them by container for distribution to needy children. In America, there is a charity called Samaritan's Purse, and one of the schemes they promote is *"a shoebox for Christmas"*. They ask people, especially youngsters, to fill a shoebox with gifts suitable for a child in age ranges 0-3, 3-6, 6-13, and over 13. Samaritan's Purse then collect the shoeboxes together and send them by container to needy countries. Unfortunately, many of the boxes have been marked *"for a cold climate"* which is hardly the case here! It is inappropriate and extravagant to give the contents of one whole shoebox to each child here in Madagascar, where the children have so little to begin with. Many of the gifts are also suitable for adult staff at the hospital.

Hence, Sheila has been asked to open each shoebox and sort the gifts out into like things. So there is a box for toothbrushes and toothpaste, for combs, pencils, rubbers, paper, toy cars, puzzles, books, toys, clothes, torches and batteries (very useful here), cuddly toys, etc, etc.

Unfortunately, some of the gifts are inappropriate – a toy moon buggy is pretty meaningless to a Malagasy child who is used to ox carts and will have never seen pictures of a moon buggy; and they will not understand the dinosaur craze, or things generated by films or television. Other gifts are clearly second hand and unwanted – this is not really the spirit of true giving, which should have an element of sacrifice. And a surprising number of things taken from hotels are sent – such as Gideon Bibles, soap, shampoo, etc. together with free samples! There are seven very large cardboard boxes, each containing around 16-20 shoeboxes to be unpacked. An exciting job seeing what is coming next, but very time consuming.

We are all exhausted from the day's events, and Johan has supper on his own. We go to bed early, at 9.30pm, but I have a bad night, waking several times. In the early morning the wind is blowing a gale through our open bedroom window, and I feel cold with only a sheet over me! Quite amazing, as I'm sure the temperature is in the 70's!!

~ • ~

Day 15: Tuesday 5th November 1996

The day dawns with overcast skies, the clouds heavy and dark in the distance. To the east, it is clearly raining over the mountains, but the rains have yet to arrive in Mandritsara. The river bed that we cross on our way to the hospital was pretty dry when we came, with just a few pools of very muddy water in low-lying places. Now, even those have dried out, the mud cracked in the heat of the sun.

We expect today to be busy for Phase 2 at the hospital. We need to concrete the footings for the laundry building and commence the excavations for the ward block foundations. At the laundry and wash area, we use the existing level of the foundations to the external wall as our level for excavation, but find that the ground is extremely hard. We really need rock drills or road breakers to do the job properly, not just picks and shovels. In fact, in places we have not been able to get down to formation level due to encountering rock, so I instruct stepped foundations to be installed.

Digging the ward block foundations　　*The ward block foundations
from the water tower*

Concreting is started at 8am, with everything being done by hand. At least this time they are using a proper gauge box, so the mix is fairly accurate. We have reduced the proportions from 1:3:6 to 1:3:5 because the aggregate is very angular and larger than it ought to be (it should be 25mm, but is probably up to 40mm). The other problem is that there is a tendency to use too much water to make it easier to place, which results in the water floating on the top as they transport it in the wheelbarrow!

Annie tells us that she has just tested Dr Hanitra for malaria, which has proved positive. She is shivering, but refuses to return home until lunch time. True to form, doctors make the worst patients, she even refuses to start treatment immediately, even though this is the instruction she herself gives out to her patients. She must take four chloroquine tablets immediately, and another four after eight hours. They are extremely bitter and make you feel nauseous, so I can understand her reluctance. In addition to two daily tablets of proguanil, we take two of these tablets weekly as a prophylactic, and that is bad enough.

As Johan and I complete the setting out for the veranda and walkway area to the ward, we have an unexpected visitor. Sheila has arrived with Beatrice, and is using the opportunity to take some more photographs, particularly of me at work. She also takes pictures of the staff working, and a young girl having a dressing changed by the nurses.

Today a new medical student has started work at HVM, and Dr Adrien brings her round to introduce her to everyone. She is a 4th year student, and is the daughter of a local pastor, the Principal of the Theological College in Mandritsara. So it is very convenient for her to get her medical practice training at HVM.

Beatrice is on holiday from today, and is flying to Majunga by Air Madagascar, due out at 12.55. During the morning she takes her luggage to the Air Mad office in town, and Sheila is surprised to see a live duck in a sewn-up basket with just its head sticking out, waiting with all the luggage to take the same flight. We all go down to the airstrip to see her off, and hear the plane coming as we leave the house. As we drive past the end of the runway it taxies towards us, a twin engine aircraft seating about 20 people. There are quite a few people there to meet the plane, and four or five *"vazahas"* get off – they are Frenchmen working with Colas, who are building a dam nearby and are also involved in road improvements.

Majunga is on the north-west coast, and Bea is meeting her Swiss friend Doris there tomorrow, when she flies in from Tana after staying with Emil and Margaret Kundig for a few days. From there they will fly to Nosy Be (*"Big Island"*), a popular tourist spot, then Diego and other places on the west and north coasts. It should be a good break for them both. They will return to Mandritsara the weekend before we depart on the Wednesday and will fly back to Tana with us, as Doris leaves Madagascar the day after us.

We return to the house for lunch of pork chops, courgettes, tomatoes, onions and rice; followed by angel delight.

Air Mad flight arriving at Mandritsara

In the afternoon, one of the temporary workers helping to excavate the foundations for the ward block hits his toe with the sharp narrow blade of the special shaped long-handled spade he is using. He is lucky not to lose his toe – he works barefoot, as the majority of the locals do. He receives treatment at the hospital, and I am amazed to find him back at work when I check on progress towards the end of the day! He is limping with his toe heavily bandaged, and has been put onto light work – removing the spoil by wheelbarrow.

Dr Jeannine is keen to have the oxygen machines working for the operating theatre, so part of the afternoon is set aside for this purpose. From her work in France, she is used to using modern, high tech equipment, and the ones HVM have been given are far from that. They are second-hand American machines, and a new plug has first to be fitted and a transformer used to step down the voltage.

After starting it up and following the instructions printed on the machine, we soon have it up and running, to Jeannine's great delight. She is still concerned, however, to know what the warning lights and sounds are for and how they operate. The main concern is that there is no humidifier bottle to fix to the machine for the oxygen to pass through. The machine makes it clear, however, that this is optional. Johan is confident that he will be able to adapt a bottle to suit, if necessary. Use of the machine is an important step in being able to provide surgical facilities.

On our way home from work, we search the town for a tractor and trailer to haul the aggregate we have ordered from a local village to the hospital. The first one we see and make enquiries about is not available until Friday, and they ask for quite a lot of money. We look for another but in vain. The one Johan used previously, and which can carry the most load, is broken down and hence not available.

Fortunately, the very next morning Johan spots one of the tractor owners at the hospital waiting for treatment, and manages to persuade him to hire out his tractor on Thursday, at a reasonable cost. His trailer is also a good size, carrying about four tonnes of material. It is a difficult time of the year to hire tractors and trailers, because the owners can make more money from transporting rice.

Supper is fresh bread, pate, cheese and salad.

As we get into bed, we hear Johan shouting for Sheila – a phone call from her mum. A pleasant surprise, and she informs us that Grenville is planning to ring us tomorrow evening and will tape the conversation for next Sunday's service in Newbury. We will have to try and stay up a bit later tomorrow night.

~ • ~

Day 16: Wednesday 6th November 1996

Sheila is up very early this morning so that she and Annie can go to the market at 7.15am before Annie goes to work. They buy lettuce, spring onions, tomatoes, paw paw, mangoes and silk bananas, all very fresh.

After setting out profile boards for the excavation of the footings for the ward block, Johan and I look at the quantities of materials we will need to complete the first part of this second phase. This consists of the foundations up to ground level for the autoclave, laundry and wash area, ward block and walkway, and a two-family (semi-detached) bungalow for medical staff. It is felt that these buildings are the minimum facilities necessary to commence regular surgical procedures.

It soon becomes apparent that there are two problems: firstly, obtaining enough aggregate for the concrete required in the short time available at the rate it is being produced; and secondly, that there is not enough money available for all that needs to be done. Money has to be found, not just for the materials and labour for the foundations, but to buy the bricks and have them delivered before the rainy season begins at the end of December.

None of the material is delivered – Johan has to find and pay for the transport separately. This is a problem in itself as there is little transport available and it is often busy carrying rice. He is very keen to provide their own transport by buying a tractor and trailer in Europe and also a Unimog truck so that he is not dependant on local transport.

Lunch is lamb chops with carrots, cauliflower and mashed potatoes, followed by fresh mangoes.

Johan and I decide that we should spend the afternoon looking for materials and seeing what is available. After lunch, as we drive away from the house to head out of town, Johan realises that he does not have the car papers with him. On each road out of town two policemen stop each car and ensure that all the papers are in order. Fortunately, on the way out the police are busy with a truck so we pass straight through, and on our return, Johan gives them a cheery wave, and they just wave back in return!

Our first visit is to the new generator building being built for the electricity company, to look at the concrete louvre panels they have built to provide ventilation to the equipment, but which prevents people looking in. A similar system is needed for the autoclave building, in which the sterilisation equipment operates at high temperatures and pressures. The standard of finish of the concrete works and the building in general is of good quality, and looking at the foundations they are laying, ours will be more than sufficient.

We then head out of town towards Befandrana in a north-westerly direction, to look for the Colas site. They are building a small dam across the river Sofia, which is very low at this time of year. After the rains, it will be in full spate, quite deep and impassable. About 4 km outside of town, the road climbs steeply and winds through a pass in the mountain range. As we start the descent on the other side, we can see clouds of dust as the Colas trucks wend their way along the purpose-built tracks to the dam site. About 4 km further on we come to the track leading to the site and make our way through a village until we reach the worksite area, parking up beside a number of containers used as the offices and stores. Each is covered in palm tree fronds to reduce the heat inside.

As we step out of the pick-up, we are enveloped in clouds of dust – we have trodden in dust lying about two inches thick on the ground! My shoes and socks get covered. In the office, we see the supervisor in charge, and Johan asks him if they have aggregate available for sale. Their crusher is about 140 km away, and we need almost 100m³ – approximately eight lorry loads. He says he will ask his superiors in Tana and let us know that evening – he is staying in a hotel in Mandritsara. It is called a hotel, but is not what we would expect of a hotel or even a guest house in England.

The news is not good. They are reluctant to let us have some of their aggregate because their stocks are low, and the price is 180,000 *fmg* (£30) per cubic metre, a total cost of 18 million *fmg* (£3,000), more than we have for everything at present. This price is almost double the cost of buying it locally, but does include transport.

We take the opportunity to have a look around the site. It is not a big dam, the crest only appears to be about a metre above the existing river level, so perhaps it is just for flood control rather than a reservoir. The site seems well organised and they have a useful batcher / concrete mixer, about 1m³ capacity. Much of the work is done by hand, but the important things by machine. Johan and I discuss the merits of HVM obtaining a concrete mixer, which I believe is essential for good concrete quality control. At the moment the quality is very hit and miss, some good but some bad.

We make our way back, following another track which leads to an area of more Colas activity. They are building a road, with a bridge that looks too good to be temporary, and Johan cannot work out what they are building it for. If it is going to cross the river it will prove advantageous to the work of HVM, because in the rainy season it is impossible to cross the river to get to some of the villages for inoculations and evangelism.

·

We return to Mandritsara, but turn off before we enter the main town, towards the village where our aggregate is being produced. As we pass through the first village, we see Pastor Julien and his wife in their new home – they have just moved here. Johan converses in Malagache and they decide that I will preach at the Church this Sunday morning, if Adrien is available to interpret.

Further along the road are lots of different brick-making facilities – stacks of bricks and brick kilns, some precariously balanced piles, and others looking much better structures. We stop and begin to look at the bricks to see if any will be suitable, and are surprised when a slight woman appears from behind the pile of bricks where she has been resting. Unfortunately the majority of the bricks are not the right size – we need to build a double skin wall with a 10mm mortar joint between each face. Most of the local bricks have their length exactly twice their width, because when they build they do not use mortar between the bricks!

We do not find any suitable, but by the time we return on the road later, some more samples are available, which we take back with us, much to the consternation of their owners, who expect payment!

The track winds on until it reaches a village of mud huts with thatched roofs. The whole of its village, containing between 15 and 20 families, is involved in stone breaking. The men produce the large stones, while the women sit all day hammering away to produce the aggregate we require, sized about 25mm down.

They had told us they had produced about 150 daba out of the 300 daba (6m³) Johan had initially ordered. In fact, looking around, there is probably only about 80 daba available, and some of the aggregate is larger than we require. If it is too large and angular, it is much more difficult to place, because the concrete has lower workability.

The women are of varying ages, from teenagers up to a couple of old women who carry on working even though the others stop to gather around us. I ask if I can take a photograph of them, and they quickly make themselves presentable, laughing as excitedly as children.

Breaking stone into aggregate for concrete

It is in this village l see a lizard about 9" long on the mud wall of a hut. I take a picture, but I'm not sure it will come out very well because it is well camouflaged and the background is dark. There is also nothing to compare its enormous length to.

In the evening is the weekly prayer meeting. It is not quite a full complement because Beatrice is on holiday and Hanitra is still recovering from her bout of malaria. After the meeting, Adrien asks if I can speak to the weekly staff meeting of HVM on Thursday. So I will be preaching on Sunday, leading devotions for the prayer meeting on Wednesday, and speaking on Thursday. A busy week ahead! Adrien wants both Sheila and myself at the hospital on Thursday to answer questions after I have brought a message.

Then at about 9.15pm local time (6.15pm GMT), Grenville rings. It is a clear line, and we put the phone on "speaker" so that we can both hear what is being said. It is being taped for the Sunday evening service, so it is imperative that we answer concisely but still need to give information. It seems to go very well, as the time lag problem is not as apparent as it sometimes is, when both parties try to speak simultaneously, then compensate by pausing together, and so on.

It is very good to hear from Newbury and know that we are being remembered. Grenville closes with a prayer, and we value the thoughts and prayers of people back home as we try to complete the task we have been set. And so to bed after another long and eventful day.

~ • ~

Day 17: Thursday 7th November 1996

We did not get time yesterday afternoon to collect the timber planks from town as planned, so we decide to go straight to the warehouse to take them to the hospital with us. It is already open, and Monsieur Azad is inside supervising one of his men painting steel hand ploughs. He has something like 30 or 40 of them there, just delivered from Tana, and are made for pulling by the zebu, the cattle that everyone has around here. Traditionally, the farmers use timber ploughs, but these metal ploughs have only been available since 1991, when the road opened from Tana, and there is quite a market for them.

During Johan's conversation with Azad, which ranges from the high cost of transport to his mark-up on the goods he sells, Johan discusses the possibility of using the warehouse for church services on Sundays, as the existing building will soon not be available. It remains an outside option.

We select five timber planks, each 40-50 mm thick and very long. Azad's men load them onto the back of the pick-up, and they look rather precarious, hanging out over the back. I offer to ride in the back to support them and we discuss briefly whether I should drive. However, it is market day and that attracts a lot of people from the villages who are not used to motor vehicles and act unpredictably. So I climb into the back and stand on the planks to keep them down.

Each time the Toyota goes over a bump, so the planks jump in the air, and gradually one of the planks moves sideways until it is in danger of hitting something at the side of the road. So I shout to Johan to stop, which he does rather suddenly! The timbers rise in the air, me with them, and they end up in a heap in the road. Fortunately I manage to jump clear. All Johan sees is a pair of legs disappearing and he thinks I have ended up on the roof.

We re-pack the timbers, this time with the planks resting on the roof of the pick-up. As we drive away, an ox cart tries to avoid the car and the oxen go out of control, crashing into the fence of a house by the side of the road. The residents come out of the house to see what has happened, shrug their shoulders, and go back in. *C'est la vie!*

Johan drives very slowly, and it is one of the longest and hairiest journeys I have done, trying to stop five heavy planks sliding off the roof of a pick-up! I am very glad when we arrive at the hospital in one piece.

We have a wide-ranging discussion in the maintenance office at the hospital. Firstly we discuss the presidential election. It looks as though the last but one President is ahead on votes at the moment, but unfortunately he is a Marxist, so there could be a time of political and religious uncertainty ahead. We go on to think about politics in Britain and Belgium, the involvement of Christians in politics, and the judiciary system in Belgium that the general population is trying to reform.

Our main discussion, however, centres on the finance requirement for Phase 2. We calculate that 13 percent of Phase 1 costs went on the foundations. This means that something like 65 million *fmg* is needed for Phase 2 (£10,000+!) and roughly a third of this for Section 1 (around £3,500). In addition, Johan really needs to order all the bricks for the Phase 2 buildings and have them delivered before the rainy season. This is a real concern, and I can tell that Johan is a little down because of this. Even when the Contract with the European Community is signed, the cash flow will cause problems. Thirty percent of the money will be paid by the E.C. to start work, but any work up to the signing is not included for payment, and a considerable amount of that 30 percent is taken by MSAADA for their fees. The second payment will not be made until 15 percent of the work has been completed, which basically means the laundry and first ward block completed.

We have been invited to lunch with Olivier and Ravo today, so we leave work slightly early so that I can change out of my work clothes. They are an extremely hospitable couple and really push the boat out with the meal they provide. As we arrive, we are offered cold drinks of coke or a home-made fruit drink, made from something like a large breadfruit.

The first course is a very colourful vegetable salad, consisting of carrots, beetroot, potatoes, green beans, tomatoes, onions and boiled eggs, all finely diced. To follow is a dish of chicken pieces in a mildly spiced sauce, with the obligatory rice. Dessert is a delicious mango and banana fresh fruit salad tossed in home-made yoghurt. We are sure this is the end of the meal, but to our surprise they bring out a large iced cake with the words *"Bonne Fete"* written across the top. It really has been an excellent meal.

Over lunch, they tell us that they come from Tamatave, a large town on the east coast. Olivier had a very good job there, but felt unfulfilled. They were desperate to have a child, but had six childless years. They felt called to the work at Hopitaly Vaovao Mahafaly in Mandritsara, and after they had responded, Ravo almost immediately fell for a child. They believe that God gave them what they most desired when they responded to His call in obedience.

Due to difficulties, their child had to be delivered by Caesarean section, and that was the very first operation carried out at the hospital in the operating theatre. It was as if God had put His seal of approval on the work. They called the baby *"Johanna"* – *"gift from God"*. What a tremendous testimony!

Olivier, Ravo and Johanna

Lunch with Olivier and Ravo

Olivier has an engaging personality, always laughing, and they are a very generous couple. At the end of the meal, quite unexpectedly, they give us a present, a souvenir to take with us to remind us of our stay. It is a large decorated cloth showing the island and places or things of interest, with the words *"Gasy ka tsara"* – *"Madagascar is good"*. It is so humbling that we who comparatively have so much, receive gifts from those who have so little but are prepared to share what they have with others. They have so much to teach us about real sacrificial giving, and there is a deep spiritual lesson for all of us.

Malagasy tablecloth

Olivier and Ravo's house is in the centre of town, near the place from which the taxi-brousses depart. We think it will be hot in the house, but in fact it is very light and airy inside. It has many rooms, and a through draught keeps things cool. Just before we leave, we are shown George the cat, who has just revealed herself to be Georgina, having just given birth to delightful kittens. They are incredibly tiny, but beautiful. We have had a marvellous time with them over lunch, and share a prayer together before we rush away.

Thursdays is the day of the HVM staff worship time and prayer meeting, from 2.15 to 2.45pm. Olivier is taking the devotions, and speaks about a woman who carries a heavy load on her head (traditional in this part of the world). A cart stops to give her a lift, but she gets on without removing the load from her head! Jesus wants us to let Him carry our burdens, but we need to be prepared to let them go. The time of prayer includes prayers for our families at home, whom they learnt about on the picnic last Friday.

After the service, Johan needs to check the water tank at the top of the water tower, as it had been leaking before he had left for furlough. Both of us climb up the outside of it, up a vertical ladder, and I take both cameras with me, one containing a slide film and the other a print film. The water tower is a concrete structure 15 metres high (about 50 feet), and has a capacity of 32,000 litres. The only way to climb it is by the vertical ladder up the outside, which is made of 8 or 10mm diameter reinforcing rods spot welded together. There are no rests, and the hoops are of such a large diameter that they would not prevent anyone falling.

However, I manage to climb the whole way in one go without stopping, and am just a little breathless at the top. It is a magnificent view from there, with all the hills around and the hospital buildings spread out beneath. It is also a good view of the progress made on the excavations for the new ward block, and Johan points out to me the area of land that belongs to HVM. I can just make out all the white posts marking the boundaries.

*Ward block foundations ready
for Ground Floor slab*

Later, we also start to snag the timber doors and windows on the Phase 1 buildings, as the supplier is chasing Johan for the release of his retention money. Snagging is carefully inspecting the work and making a list of all the defects that need to be rectified.

Johan and Annie join us for supper, and we learn that the woman from church who was taken to hospital last Sunday, and whose brother works at the hospital, is still in a coma. Annie has been to take some more blood samples, to check for diabetes. The prognosis does not look good – she is not getting enough fluids through the intravenous tube.

<hr />

CHAPTER EIGHT
A trip to Matsamena and Pont Sofia

Day 18: Friday 8th November 1996

We awake to a power cut, but fortunately it lasts only until 7.45am. We don't need to leave until 8am because Johan is on radio duty again, reporting to MAF although he has been having trouble getting through at this time. Reception varies considerably throughout the year, and it is fortunate that they are no longer so reliant on the radio, with the satellite telephone link and email capability. At the moment, though, we can only receive emails and not send. There seems to be a problem with the baud rate and trying to change the settings, which keep defaulting to settings which don't work properly.

We have a fairly busy morning and are just putting marker pegs to clear the vegetation from the area of the two-family accommodation, when Dr Jeannine asks Johan if he can transport a seriously ill patient to the Government hospital. It is after 11.30am, so we will take an early lunch. We drive the pick-up to the front of the hospital to find the patient, a middle-aged man, lying hunched in the recovery position on a trolley. Two of the hospital staff and his sons carry him to the Toyota and with great difficulty put him inside. It is not an ambulance and really is not suitable for transporting people like this. The man is moaning and groaning in pain which increases every time we go over a bump along the dirt road – every few hundred yards!

On arrival at the Government hospital, the patient's family

refuse to get him out – they say he has already been there and they weren't able to help him, and that is why he went to HVM in the first place! They want Johan to take them to a house near the airstrip, where they have relatives, and they will pay for a private doctor to visit. There is little that any other doctor will be able to do that cannot be done by the Government hospital or HVM, but they do not understand this. Johan is a little upset because he is being used as a taxi service.

He ought to be given medical staff if people are being transported, and he can ill afford the time for these activities. We discover later that the man has suspected hepatitis, so we hope we have not had contact that could lead to us catching it!

Lunch is spaghetti bolognaise followed by banana. We can't have too many bananas, they are so plentiful and cheap, and taste so much better than at home.

In the afternoon, Sheila walks into town to visit Dr Hanitra, who is off sick with malaria. I had seen her at work yesterday morning but she had a bad headache and was not really recovered so had returned home. Today, however, she is feeling much better and is doing some washing. She is not really able to entertain, as she has only one room in which to sleep, cook and eat, etc. with her sink on the veranda outside. To cook she has a primus stove. The room simply has a bed, a table and chair. The bathroom and toilet is shared with Dr Jeannine. How important it is for us to get the second house built at the hospital – it is intended for the doctors, together with Beatrice and Annie.

Hanitra's English has improved with practice, in speaking to Sheila. She is reluctant to speak it, not thinking it good enough, but Sheila can understand her well. On Sheila's journey home, she is joined by a number of small children, who take her hand as she walks along.

As we prepare to go out to eat in the evening, Fabien turns up to see Johan. He is a teacher and can also speak good English. He is due to read the lesson on Sunday, so wants the reading from me.

We go out to the Restaurant Belle Vue for our special weekly treat – steak and chips. The steak is marinated in ginger and lime juice, and the chips are fried in peanut oil. The meal is delicious, but it is the first restaurant I have been where you have to order your meal a few days in advance; take your own candles (no electric lighting); your own ketchup and filtered water; and take your empty coke bottles for a refill. All part of life's rich tapestry!

Friday night is also video night! So after the meal we congregate in Johan's to select and watch a suitable film. We decide on a tense thriller, and Annie really gets involved, getting all worked up as the suspense builds. It is good entertainment watching her! She complains that they always seem to watch the scary films when she is on her own upstairs, with Beatrice away!

We can hardly stay awake for the end of the film, and fall into bed exhausted.

Restaurant Belle Vue

~ • ~

Day 19: Saturday 9th November 1996

Annie has planned to take us on a trip out to the villages in David Mann's Land Rover. Pastor Julien has asked either Johan or Annie to take him and some church workers to the village of Matsamena, some 40 km away. They want to go to chop and cut wood to be able to build their own church building, to reduce their dependence on renting other people's property and avoid the problems that they are having at the moment, trying to find somewhere to meet.

Apart from the three of us, the church has been told there is room for seven others. Unfortunately, 12 people, including the Pastor, turn up, some girls amongst them who apparently are going to cook lunch for the men. So there is a delay while they sort out exactly who will go, and it takes quite a time to load up the barrels of water and tie them to the roof, and sort out what bags and cooking utensils can be taken. At the same time Johan checks the Land Rover over, and tops up the diesel to ensure we don't run out. Instead of an 8am departure, we eventually leave at 8.30 and have an almost immediate stop to allow the pastor to buy some food in the market.

As soon as we get out onto the open road, the two girls and three men in the back start singing songs and hymns in harmony. Whilst their singing is very tuneful, the girls tend to shout a little and it can sound a little shrill. Their memories are extremely good, they don't need words, and they do not normally have music in Church so that is not a problem either. The singing goes on non-stop for the whole journey to Matsamena, which takes about an hour.

The road twists and winds with some very sharp and dangerous bends in places. It appears that Colas are building a new road close to the existing one along part of the route, to remove some of the bends. When we arrive in the village of Matsamena, there are just a few women about, selling fruit and sugar bricks by the side of the main road. Pastor Julien goes to find the Christian man who is to show them where they can cut timber for the new church.

When they appear, we discover he has been making sugar bricks so we are invited to see the process. It is taking place at the far end of the village, and we pass the village church on our way. All the buildings in the village are constructed with a timber frame, infilled with mud-daubed walls and roots of dried grass and raffia, just like thatch.

The sugar cane is cut and stripped, and rolled between two large logs to squeeze out all the juice. A channel has been cut in the lower log to direct the juice into a flat pan like a wok. This is then boiled over a charcoal fire while it solidifies and it is put into a mould which has the producer's initials carved into it. This is then sun dried and when struck from the mould produces a block of sugar about the size of a house brick, which is extremely hard and quite heavy. We are very privileged to be given a brick as a souvenir. These people are quite poor, yet are prepared to be so generous.

Sugar brick made in Matsamena

Annie leaves us in the village while she drives the workers to cut the timber, and gradually, as the word gets around, more and more children turn up to see the curiosities in their village – *"vazahas"*. Everywhere we go, the vast majority of people are happy for us to take their photographs, and here is no exception.

We see a woman pounding rice, with her child close by, also pounding. Sheila has a go, and the women have great delight in telling the others about her weak efforts! It is surprisingly hard work. Then Sheila tries to winnow the rice in a shallow basket, again to great amusement, and all recorded on camera.

Pounding rice in Matsamena   *Sheila attempting to winnow rice*

An old woman is weaving a mat with raffia, very intricate work. As we watch, the hordes of children following us crowd around her. At this she unleashes a torrent of words at the children, no doubt telling them to go away and keep out of her way. The children just smile and carry on regardless.

Matsamena village   *Typical village dwellings*

Annie returns and we leave the village to the happy sound of the children's laughter and their waves goodbye. We are heading further on to Farara, about 7 or 8 km away. On a Saturday, this is a busy, bustling place, full of market activity and lots of people. It simply consists of a market about ¾ mile long either side of the main road.

We drive right through the village to park on the far side. We have difficulty getting through due to the press of people and the habit of taxi brousses just stopping to let their passengers off or have a chat, in the centre of the road. We park up by the side of the road and have a bun and coffee before venturing into the market.

First of all we make our way to where produce is being sold, and buy ten large bananas for 1,000 *fmg* (16p). They cannot believe how much we pay for them at home. We then try and buy a piece of cloth with the words Madagascar and the map of the island printed on it, but although it is only 10.30am, a lot of the stalls are already starting to pack up.

We continue on our journey, heading for the Pont Sofia – a large steel girder bridge over the river Sofia which runs past Mandritsara from the mountains in the north and west. On the whole journey from Tana to Mandritsara, this is some of the most beautiful countryside to be seen. We pass through green and fertile areas, lakes being fished by men wading with nets in water waist deep, trees and wooded areas, while all around is the backdrop of mountain ranges and rocky outcrops.

There are no public toilets, of course, so on long journeys it is necessary to just pull up and find a suitable tree or shrub in the bush. Apparently the locals have no embarrassment about this, because it is common to come across a taxi brousse stopped, with all its passengers lined up on the side of the road, relieving themselves.

We reach the Pont Sofia, some 80 km from Mandritsara, after a total drive time of two hours. It was built in the 1960's from steel made in Lille, France. An ox cart is crossing it when we arrive, and we walk across. The view of the river and surrounding hills and mountains is breathtaking, even though the river is very low, with lots of sandbanks breaking through. In a short time, when the rains come, it will be a raging torrent.

From the bridge we return a short way along the road to a suitable place on the river bank and in the shade of huge mango trees, to eat the picnic lunch of pizza followed by banana and coffee which Annie has provided. Zebu are grazing nearby, and one wades into the shallow water just in front of us to eat the fallen mangoes. The juice runs out of the sides of its mouth as it slowly chews them, and we hear crunching noises as it tries to eat the hard stones. Eventually it gives up and with a great effort swallows the stone whole.

Our siesta is soon spoilt by a group of four or five youths. Two of them are hunting for beetles, digging a shallow hole and threading the caught insect on a stick – apparently quite a delicacy. The ground is soon peppered with holes and disturbed ground. The others have sticks and are throwing them with great accuracy high into the trees to hit the ripe mangoes, which fall with a thud to the ground.

Soon it is time for us to leave for the return journey. At Farara, the market is cleared away and the town looks almost empty. We take the track off the main road down to the river, a very sandy and rutted route. At the river a number of people are bathing or washing clothes. There is a crossing of sorts, although I would be reluctant to drive a vehicle over it. It is made of timber, with dried grass and mud holding it all together. In many places, this is missing, and just the framework is showing. It apparently gets washed away in the rainy season and repeatedly needs replacing. The amazing thing is that the hospital staff regularly have to take this route when they visit the outlying villages for inoculations and evangelism.

We arrive back at Matsamena at 3.45, a quarter of an hour early. Two of the workers are here, the work apparently having finished. We proceed to where Annie dropped the workers off, to collect the rest. The timber has been hidden for collection on another occasion, but they have a number of large fruits to take back with them.

On the return, the singers decide to practice their repertoire of hymns and songs in English, as much as they know, and we are able to join in with some of them, to their great delight. We had hoped they will be too tired to sing on the way back, but they keep going all the way. Just outside Mandritsara, Julien asks Annie to stop the car, and two of the young people pray, giving thanks for the day.

We arrive home, hot, tired and dusty just before 5pm. As we unpack the car, Annie's container with the remains of her pizza falls to the floor. One of the youngsters picks it up, and asks me a question, which I answer in the affirmative, saying *"Yes, it's pizza"*. They think I am giving them permission to eat it, which they promptly do before anyone can stop them. Poor Annie, she thought it would last another meal.

Before we have had a chance to shower and freshen up, Adrien comes round to ask about tomorrow's service. He is translating for me, and needs to have a rough idea of what I will be saying to make it easier for him.

Johan, Sheila and myself decide to go to the Restaurant Belle Vue again, to try the *soup speciale* (a Chinese soup with noodles and meat – very filling) and *Riz Cantonese* – rice with chicken, spring onion, and chopped vegetables. Fortunately, this meal doesn't have to be ordered beforehand, as they are local dishes. Apart from the grit I encounter in the rice, it is very good but too much – none of us is able to finish the meal. The cost, a total of 6,000 *fmg* (£1) per head! On our return to the house, Johan checks on the emails. There are two for us – one from Philip and one from International Office, sent yesterday.

~ • ~

Day 20: Sunday 10th November 1996

I am preaching today, so have to sit at the front of the church, in full view at the side, on a bench with Adrien, Fabien and Pastor Julien, who leads the service. In front of us are 80 to 100 of the younger children sat on mats on the floor. The congregation is on our left, sat on pews. The choir sits in the front few rows on our side of the church, and the older children sit at the front on the opposite side. The church building is full, and there are more children than adults. They really try to make us feel at home, and have chosen some of the hymns that we will know, for example,

"*O for a thousand tongues*":
"*My lanitra ao ambony ao,*
  Andriananita o!
  Izay rehetra vitanao
  Dia mahagaga anay"

and a nationalistic song to the tune of *"God Save our Queen"*.

The children's talk is about Zaccheus and they sing *"Shine Jesus Shine"* with great verve. The service starts slightly late at 8.40am and I start preaching at about 9.30 on the subject *"Following"*, which with interpretation, takes half an hour. I am very wary and nervous about how it will go, because the sermon inevitably becomes disjointed, and there is the danger of the interpreter not understanding some of the words or phrases. I try to avoid idioms and difficult words, and Adrien is very good. Just once or twice he has to ask me what something means, and it seems to flow fairly well. It is difficult to get into a rhythm at first because Malagasy has many more words than the English equivalent, but it soon becomes easier.

The service ends soon after 10.30 and we then go outside to shake hands. It seems to go on forever, with all the children first, followed by the adults and finally the choir. There is hardly room outside for the spiral of people as each person shakes everyone's hand. The number of times I have to repeat *"Saloma tempoko"*, although many try to say *"Good morning"* and *"Thank you"*.

We go back inside for communion. After prayers and one verse of a hymn, we are served with a piece of biscuit, which has to be retained for all to eat together. Then the wine is some sort of fruit juice, served in small plastic cups, again drunk together. The two servers (one is Flavien from the hospital) give thanks for the bread and wine.

Following the church service, a lot of members go to the Government hospital to pray for the young woman that Johan took to hospital last Sunday, the sister of one of HVM's workers and the daughter of the church choirmaster. The doctors do not know what is wrong with her, she is still in a coma, and the prognosis does not look good. In their prayers, it is apparent that the family have accepted that she may not recover.

Sunday school

Long queue for greeting everyone after church

Sheila then works hard to produce a typical English Sunday lunch for the four of us. We have roast lamb with onion sauce, roast potatoes, carrots, green beans, cauliflower and Yorkshire pudding. To follow is lemon meringue pie. Delicious!

Annie has made a drink with fresh lemons, which is very refreshing.

They have discovered the mail in the suitcase that arrived by truck from Tana that morning, so there is great excitement for Johan and Annie as they open letters from friends and family. It is scenes like this that make you realise how far away missionaries are, and how they depend and really look forward to correspondence and news from back home. We have a good time of fellowship together with wide-ranging discussions, particularly concerning AEF, and personnel that we know.

At dusk, we see four people coming from the hospital and carrying a dead person on their shoulders like pall bearers. It is traditional for the body to be removed to the family home for a wake to begin, so that friends can come to the house and pay their respects. The burial then takes place the following day.

In the evening we meet together again for a special prayer meeting called by the AEF International Board. They have requested wisdom for AEF's vision, role, purpose and future development, etc. in a changing situation. It is a good time of open and frank discussion and exchange of views interspersed with times of intercession.

～ • ～

Day 21: Monday 11th November 1996

After three weeks we finally succumb to our first (and only, I hope!) bout of stomach trouble. During the night, Sheila starts with diarrhoea and stomach cramps, and a couple of hours later I start, but less severe. I get up reasonably early and recover during the morning, but Sheila has to stay in bed and has a bad head and 'flu-like symptoms. Johan and Annie are both OK, and we all ate basically the same yesterday, so I'm not sure what it can have been. I miss work this morning, but at least it gives me the opportunity to prepare my talks for Wednesday night and Thursday afternoon.

I feel fit enough to accompany Johan to work in the afternoon, but Sheila is still laid low in bed. She has stopped going to the loo, but is worn out and aches, perhaps gastric 'flu. After quickly checking progress on the concreting of the foundations to the east end of the ward block, the rest of the afternoon is spent setting out the house. I have told Johan that as a practical exercise, he is to set it out from start to finish. So he has been busy over the weekend, planning what to do and drawing a sketch of the foundations with dimensions so that it can be marked out. I check his calculations and find out step-by-step the way he plans to proceed, giving some advice on the way.

We establish our baseline from the existing house, which is intended for David and Jane Mann, and he has to set up the theodolite over the setting out point we have established. It is sometimes quite difficult to stand back and watch someone make mistakes and take much longer than you think is necessary, but it is very important to let people get practice. The only way to become proficient at anything is to keep practising.

Another thing that slows everything up is that Johan is taking notes of everything we do, each step in the procedure so that in six months' time when he has forgotten all I told him, he can refer back to his notes. I must learn to have more patience. The problem is, I know how little time there is remaining until we return, and so much I still want to do.

On our return from work, Sheila is still not well and I make our supper of scrambled eggs and ham. She has a visit this afternoon from Gisele to see how she is, but it tires her out and she has to return to bed. Hopefully, after a good night's rest, she will feel much better and able to go to the market tomorrow as arranged.

～ • ～

CHAPTER NINE
Leading Devotions

Day 22: Tuesday 12th November 1996

Tuesday morning is the time to post the air mail letters at the Post Office in Mandritsara to catch the weekly Air Madagascar flight to Tana. This week the flight has been cancelled, but Johan takes one of his letters on the way to work and asks whether the post will be going. He is told that there will be a flight this morning, but to and from Majunga, so the mail will leave on this flight.

We then went to visit another Monsieur Azad, who has a concrete mixer that we would like to hire. He lives in a large house with a huge workshop and yard, off the area in the centre of town where all the ox carts park. We see the concrete mixer, a large, well-used machine with a diesel motor, of ⅓ m³ capacity. It does not have tyres and is well coated with old concrete and what looks like an old car tyre as the drive belt. Monsieur Azad's wife, the owner of the building housing the HVM clinic adjacent to the air strip, leads us up the stairs to their living quarters. She asks us to take a seat on the long and wide veranda, while she goes to fetch her husband. He is a short man, as wide as he is tall, and appears to roll along the veranda.

Johan gets down to business by trying to persuade them (in French) to allow us to use the mixer. Eventually, they state their price of 100,000 *fmg* per day, saying that Colas had to hire it for 300,000 *fmg* per day! Johan responds that Colas has plenty of money but HVM has none. I ask Johan if their price is negotiable, which I don't think has occurred to him. So he informs the Azads that his guest says that we should negotiate the price, as surely that is the custom in Madagascar? That causes them great amusement and immediately reduce the asking price to 80,000 *fmg* per day (about £13) which we accept.

We calculate that because less labour will be required and mixing will be considerably quicker, we should be able to save at least that amount, so the mixer will pay for itself. The next problem is transporting it to the hospital. Its days of being towed were long over. Johan backs his pick-up into the yard adjacent to the mixer, which causes great amusement to the labourers there, as they can see there was no way it will take it. So Monsieur Azad offers to load it onto his truck and bring it to the hospital in 15 minutes time. He has 15-20 men there to manhandle it, but it is about two hours before it actually arrives. We are relieved it is no longer our problem and make a hasty retreat.

As we come out of the yard, we find a group of about a dozen prisoners from the local jail, accompanied by a solitary warder. They are about to form a working party, and are armed with a variety of tools. It is apparently quite common to see prisoners out and about, helping where possible, and anyone can hire them as cheap labour. I suddenly remember that we have left cameras in the pick-up, and am relieved to find they are untouched. I then feel guilty that I should have suspected that they might be taken.

When it does arrive, accompanied by Madame Azad, we have the lesser problem of off-loading the mixer, and manage to slide it down planks after a considerable amount of effort. Then, of course, the diesel engine has not been started for a long time, so a further half an hour is wasted, tinkering with it until it fires with a blast of black exhaust. It is all supervised by Madame Azad, anxious to ensure that no harm comes to it.

It proves its worth in the first hour of use, however, as the concrete gang finish off the pour they had started at 5.00am. Our next problem will be obtaining enough materials to keep up with its rate of producing the concrete. We are almost out of sand, because the tractor and trailer have not been available to transport it. The sand is dug from the river bed, and this time of the year it gets harder and harder to obtain, because they have to go very deep and the sand is very soft, so they cannot get the tractor and trailer close enough. In the rainy season the sand gets replenished, but of course it is unobtainable then. The best time of the year to dig sand is between June and September.

On our arrival at the site after our successful negotiations with the Azads, I see yet another example of the Malagasy ingenuity and inventiveness. Idoxy's husband, Bienvenue, is repairing and sharpening tools such as cold chisels, picks, etc and has lit a charcoal fire surrounded on three sides by bricks with the steel tools going red-hot in the fire. Behind the bricks are arranged a few granite blocks, supporting two vertical cylindrical metal tubes about 2" in diameter. In each tube is a timber rod with cloth wrapped around to fill up the space between the rod and tube. Another man sits pumping each rod up and down within the tube, so creating a draught which lights the charcoal a bright cherry red, raising the temperature enough to heat the steel. The steel is then hammered out as necessary.

Our morning is taken up with continuing the setting out of the house foundations. Each corner is marked out with pegs but on checking the diagonals there is an error, showing it is out of square. While Johan returns home to receive a radio message that he had been told to expect yesterday, I set up the theodolite and correct the morning's work.

Annie has been taking her video camera to work for the past two days, hoping to film us using the theodolite. Late afternoon, we are to level pins to give the levels for the concrete footings to the ward block for tomorrow's concreting, so I let Annie know so that she can video the work. After finishing off what she is doing, Annie comes out and sets up her camera on its tripod, and asks me to explain on the video what we are doing. She starts to film and after about three seconds, the film runs out, so that is the end of that!

After supper that evening, she shows us her video recording of the hospital inauguration ceremony that took place last June, and of what she has filmed since we arrived, although much of this has been lost because she accidentally wound it back and filmed over it!

～ • ～

Day 23: Wednesday 13th November 1996

Outside the entrance to the hospital stands a village dwelling with a shelter that sells produce and offers refreshment to those visiting the hospital. They have a lemur as a pet, the national emblem and infamous animal of Madagascar. It is allowed to run free, and hangs from the vertical timber posts and jumps from place to place, quite unafraid of human presence. As we will not have time to visit the rain forests or any of the national parks, we do not expect to see any lemurs, so even seeing a tame one is pleasing.

Yesterday I think I upset Johan because I feel that fitting the solar panels to the roof of Phase 1 is a priority. As the money for these panels was donated by Newbury Baptist Church, I feel it is not right to return home without seeing them fitted, with suitable slides to show everyone at home what their money has provided. To ensure financial and prayer support continues, it must be clear that the recipient is grateful and using the gift.

The solar panels should have been fitted last June, and were actually assembled on the floor in the garage to make sure everything fitted together. However, Johan has serious doubts about the capability of the angle supports to carry the considerable weight of the units when filled with hot water (300 kg plus the self-weight). Also, the roof trusses are not in the right positions for the fittings. Hence the job was left, and Johan has so many other things that people want him to do, that solar panels have become very low priority.

Each staff member at HVM has their own priority for what they think Johan should be doing, and there is clearly not enough time for him to do everything. However, I'm sure the problems with the fixing of the panels can be easily overcome, but I will only discuss it if he brings the subject up again – I have had my say, and he knows my feelings.

Sheila and I decided a few days ago to invite those who have shown us hospitality to a meal at the Restaurant Belle Vue – Dr Adrien and Gisele; Olivier and Ravo; Drs Jeannine and Hanitra plus Johan, Annie and Beatrice and her friend Doris (if they are back from holiday). We leave the choice of Friday or Saturday to Adrien and Gisele because they will need to find a baby sitter. I first asked Adrien last Friday evening, and noticed a slight reluctance. When Johan spoke to him to find out if he had decided which day, he discovered that they do not like going out to the local restaurants for health reasons!

So yesterday I told Adrien that we had decided to have the meal in the Manns' residence instead. He nearly jumped for joy, delight spreading over his face until Johan teased him that we would be ordering a takeaway from the Belle Vue!

Today I have the opportunity to ask Jeannine and Hanitra, the latter accepting thankfully. Jeannine sadly informs me that she will be unable to come as she is on duty at the hospital, since they will be carrying out two operations on Friday afternoon and the doctors are required to provide some of the post-operative care on a rota basis. Dr Adrien is anxious to begin regular surgery, but others are reluctant until there are proper facilities in place. A compromise has been struck.

For most of the day, the sky is overcast and cloudy, with some of the clouds dark and menacing. We really think that the early rains will come, but even though we can see it raining on the hills all around Mandritsara, in the basin we only get a few drops at the hospital, and none back at the house. It would be so refreshing to have a shower of rain to settle all the dust. The only problem then is that the roads would probably become very slippery as the dust turns to mud!

Sitting quietly in the maintenance office doing some calculations, I hear a strange sawing noise apparently coming from the ceiling, which consists of bamboo-like timber cut in half lengthways, to produce semi-circular sections. The ceilings look quite attractive, but they are also attractive to termites, like wood-worm only on a larger scale. The noise I can hear is the termites enjoying a tasty snack. Johan needs to spray the whole area with insecticide to destroy the termites, or they will eat their way through all the timber in sight.

This evening is the weekly HVM/AEF Prayer Meeting, and I have been asked to lead the devotions. Adrien is busy translating for Ravo as I talk, but suddenly I realise there is silence – he has stopped and is looking at me blankly. I have spoken about arrows (from Isaiah 49:2) and he does not understand what I mean, so I stop and explain about bow and arrows, then light dawns. From then on, everything is fine. What a difficult task it is to translate into a language that is not even your second one, but the third – Malagasy, French, then English! He does extremely well, especially since a lot of words do not translate directly from one language to the other. The title of the hospital is a good example – we call it *"The Good News Hospital"*. They call it

"Hopitaly Vaovao Mahafaly", literally *"The hospital with news that makes people happy"*.

～ • ～

Day 24: Thursday 14th November 1996

This morning Johan and I try to leave a little early so that I can take photos of the early morning worship that takes place each day before consultations begin. True to form, however, we have to stop twice before we get there to talk to people who want to see Johan, so I arrive just before the service ends, which has been taken by Adrien.

Immediately after this evangelistic service, which lasts about 15 minutes and is a clear presentation of the gospel listened intently by all the patients, there is a further 15 minutes on a topic of health education. Today it is on the subject of intestinal worms, how to avoid them and what to do if you have them. The talk is illustrated with flannelgraph pictures and is extremely effective. The nurse giving the talk then asks for questions and explains the hospital procedure. Surgery is then ready to begin for the day.

Drs Jeaninne and Hanitra

Health lecture to out-patients after gospel service

The maid who looks after the Manns' house for them, working about 2 hours a day, is Radesana's wife. He is the storeman for the maintenance department. She does some washing up, irons any washing Sheila has done, and cleans by a strict rota given to her by

Jane Mann that she refuses to change. Today Sheila asks Gisele to explain to her that the living room needs to be thoroughly cleaned tomorrow because we're expecting a number of guests. There is some misunderstanding, however, and she insists that it needs to be done today.

You can imagine the comic scene of Sheila frantically searching through the Malagasy/English phrasebook whilst the maid is poised with feather duster. In the end, Sheila drags her off to Johan, who has returned to the house to do some AEF work. He explains to her that it is tomorrow, and not today that the cleaning needs to be done.

With Johan away from the hospital all morning, I have to supervise the work alone. Although Radesana's English is fairly good, if there are real problems, I can call on Adrien. In fact, there is little problem as Jean (the foreman) and I seem to have a good understanding without the use of words.

Concreting of the ward foundations is now well advanced, and additional sand and aggregate is collected by tractor and trailer today to keep us going. Excavation of the house foundations begin, albeit slowly because the ground is rock hard in this location. We soon learn that the secret is to dampen the ground with water along the line of the trench, and the water changes the characteristics of the soil considerably. It becomes much easier to dig and real progress can be made.

In the afternoon, immediately after lunch, is the weekly HVM staff service. It is half-an-hour of fellowship with a hymn, message and time of prayer, followed by the ubiquitous notices! Today I have been asked to bring a message to the staff, my third speaking engagement this week. As the main purpose of my visit is to build the foundations for Phase 2, I speak about our need for deep foundations on the rock, Jesus Christ, and citing the story Jesus told about the wise and foolish builders. This leads on to the use of my surveying instruments and tools to enable us to build straight and true, and in particular the plumb-line (as in Amos 7: 7-8).

Leading devotions to staff

My talk is followed by a question and answer session to Sheila and myself. The questions are very varied – ranging from the role of the monarchy in Britain to the London Underground, which they could not visualise – trains running under the ground! Jean, the building foreman, asks whether we would be returning to complete Phase 2. He hopes that I can continue to teach building techniques to them, because he has already learnt a great deal about concrete and foundations. I discover that Malagasy engineers and surveyors do not share their knowledge, in the hope that they will be regarded as indispensable. Hence Jean is surprised that I am willing to explain things to them, and teach Johan to use the survey instruments that will all be left there when I leave.

They also show a great interest in Newbury Baptist Church and their support of the hospital. We hope that this will continue when we return, because we will certainly not forget the need here and the way it is being met, both physically in the provision of medical care, and spiritually in putting the gospel message first.

When the service finishes, Sheila takes more photos of the staff and starts to hang the curtains she has managed to complete so far. She plans to bring the balance of the curtains next Tuesday when we will have to say our goodbyes.

Johan feels that the talk I have given is so appropriate that he asks me to talk to the building workers and maintenance staff tomorrow – they have a separate meeting because most of them are temporary workers and are not Christians, so the meeting is geared for them.

I start to make a list of the jobs that can be done by the maintenance and building staff when we have left.

Tonight we send our first and last emails from Mandritsara, after the fault is traced to the baud rate setting on the telephone/ modem. We send one each to Philip, John Turk and AEF International Office, because they have sent ones to us.

~ • ~

Day 25: Friday 15th November 1996

Today is a big day for HVM. Dr Adrien has planned two operations for this morning, starting at 7.00am. They are both Caesarean sections necessary for medical reasons. It is interesting as we drive past the operating theatre on our arrival, to look in the window and see everyone with gowns and masks on, performing the operation – so unlike home.

The first mother had been treated by Adrien and David Mann over the past year for kidney problems, and Adrien was very surprised when he recently met his patient and discovered she was pregnant. She very much wants to have the baby in Mandritsara, but Dr Adrien had told her this would not be possible, she would have to go to Antsohihy, 140 km away, to have a Caesarean. The family could not afford it, however, and eventually managed to persuade Adrien to carry out the operation at HVM. When the family had consulted him, they asked him about God, saying that they knew nothing about Him, and Adrien promised to speak further with them. He was delighted when the family turned up at church last Sunday.

It is as well a C-section is carried out, because the baby is the wrong way round and the cord is wrapped around its neck. They are also grateful that Johan has got the oxygen machine up and running because it proves necessary for mother and baby. Dr Jeannine's initial reluctance to operate seems to have been overcome – her confidence has now increased. The first baby delivered is a boy, who is named Fabien; the second is a girl, to be called Louise Lauren.

At about 8.30am there is a natural pause in the concreting operations as the mechanic from Monsieur Azaz is fitting a spare part to the concrete mixer. Johan decides that it is a good time to get all the workmen together and have their weekly service. Unfortunately, Flavien cannot be present because his Aunt has just died unexpectedly and he has returned to his village for the funeral.

The workers, about 20 of them, congregate in the garage and after a hymn, I give a similar message to yesterday, about the need for spiritual foundations and to live our lives straight and true like a plumb-line. The men are all extremely attentive, and the seed is sown in the hearts of those who do not profess to be Christians, which is over half of those present. Annie is filming some of it on video, so it will be interesting to watch.

There is an amusing incident during my talk, again the result of misunderstandings during translating. I make a statement and Johan translates it as a question. When he asks the question and pauses, I begin with my next sentence, and am stopped as he explains that he has turned my statement into a question. By the time it has been answered, I have completely lost my train of thought, and lose my way for a few seconds. It is amazing how easily you can be thrown by the unexpected.

Annie also videos us doing levelling for the ward block, but misses Johan slipping into one of the trenches! She always manages to stop the video camera and miss the best bits. Just outside of the village at the hospital gates, the road dips and has rice paddy fields either side. From January to May or June, this part of the road is under water, and it is very difficult for cyclists to get through, and walkers have to wade in the mud. Johan asks me to draw a suitable scheme for a footpath and cycle path to one side of the road, so we take the level and staff to see what will be necessary. The simple section I draw up shows a 100mm deep x 700 wide concrete base, with 200mm stone cubes, 3 wide, topped by a 50mm x 600 wide concrete path. We will tell Jean what needs to be done, and he will complete it when we have left, but in time for the rainy season.

We return to the house early, as Johan has AEF work to catch up with and HVM letters to write, so I take the opportunity to plan the extra room upstairs for Beatrice and Annie. During the day, they have to eat in their kitchen because it is too hot to sit out. The planned extra room is for a dining area and so that they can entertain other than in the evenings. I measure everything up, and draw the plan and sections at work during the afternoon. I also complete the snagging of David and Jane's new house in the hospital grounds, so that the list of outstanding work can be left with the workers for completion. Then, hopefully, within a few weeks of their arrival back here in January, the Manns will be able to move into their new home.

It is Johan's tenth Wedding Anniversary today, so Sheila gives him a posy of flowers, and Annie makes him a pavlova for lunch time. Now the email is finally up and running he will send his wife Ann one tonight.

I return alone to work in the Toyota pick-up in the afternoon, the plan is that Johan will follow later. Everything goes well until about 4.40pm, when I go to check on the concrete progress. The mixer is stopped and cleaned out, they are cleaning their tools and the wheelbarrows. Imagine my horror when I look in the trench and see a 5 metre length of footing where the concrete is an average of 60-70mm low.

I manage to get across to Jean that another batch of concrete is required, they cannot leave the concrete as it is. I am not very popular, especially as it is 6pm before they finish. When Johan finally arrives, he spends a considerable time explaining to them the importance of finishing the concrete to a vertical face, not horizontal. The problem is that they are a little ambitious and place the stop-end just too far to finish in the time. But they learn quickly, and are keen to please.

Also in the afternoon, Sheila rides Annie's bicycle to the Church Women's meeting where they are learning to crochet, followed by devotions. The women work in quiet, not like at home where there would be a lot of chattering. After the meeting, Gisele comes to the house to learn how to make crumble.

Church women's meeting

This evening is our special meal to thank everyone for their kind hospitality to us. So we entertain Adrien and Gisele; Olivier and Ravo (and of course they never go anywhere without daughter Johanna); Hanitra; Annie and Johan. Missing are Jeannine, on duty at the hospital, and Beatrice, due to return from her holiday tomorrow.

We have lasagne with coleslaw, rice salad, diced tomatoes and spring onions, and freshly-baked bread. This is followed by mango crumble; lemon meringue pie and lychee sorbet. The meal is accompanied by a lemon drink made from freshly squeezed fruit. After the meal everyone relaxes over coffee and Belgian chocolates (provided by Johan), and we have a really good time of fellowship. Towards the end we have an unexpected presentation. The hospital has made us a gift of beautiful embroidered curtains, decorated with a typical Malagasy scene – pounding the rice. How appropriate, considering the efforts Sheila has made in completing the hospital curtains.

~ • ~

CHAPTER TEN
A Busy Weekend

Day 26: Saturday 16th November 1996

We have arranged for the concrete gang to work on the ward block foundations this Saturday morning. As Johan is busy working on his sermon for tomorrow's service, I drive Sheila to the hospital. We were able to have a lie-in until 6.45am!! It is amazing that here you just don't seem able to stay in bed in the morning, but I bet that changes the moment we arrive home!

Sheila wants to make sure that the curtains are hung in the recovery room, where the two post-operative patients are being nursed with their babies. We are surprised to see a few patients at the hospital, but we learn that it is appointments only. As Dr Jeannine is here having spent all night on duty, and Dr Adrien has arrived to take over from her, a small clinic is held.

Sheila has great delight in visiting the two mothers and making a fuss of the babies and taking their photos, after hanging the curtains in their room to give them some privacy. I check on the concreting progress and we return to town with Olivier and Jeannine. Jeannine comments on how good it has been to have Sheila here because of the encouragement she gives and the way she is able to communicate with people, whoever they are. Gisele has made similar comments, saying she has thoroughly enjoyed having Sheila's company. She has learnt a great deal from their contact and visits to the market, etc, and her English has improved a great deal as she has been forced to practise it.

On our return we walk to the market for more tomatoes and bananas, and decide to return the long way round, on the tarmac roads. We see and buy an oil lamp which is a real lesson about recycling in our throwaway society. It has been made from an old light bulb with bits of old tin cans brazed together. It also gives us a spiritual lesson. The light bulb originally worked perfectly in the way it had been designed, but could not when the filament failed. God designed man to be perfect and to shine as His light. But sin spoilt that and our light went out. Jesus is the perfect light of the world and He enables us to be re-used as His lights if we allow ourselves to be filled with the oil of His Spirit and our wick trimmed by the action of God's words in our lives.

One important lesson I have learnt from my time here is how adaptable and flexible you have to be, and turn your hand to whatever needs doing. The six-seater MAF plane is due to land at Mandritsara at midday, after flying tourists to Nosy Be (in the north) this morning and needs to refuel. It comes to us having collected Beatrice and Doris, saving them a tiring 8-10 hours journey by taxi brousse after an Air Madagascar flight. They had been incorrectly informed there is no direct flight by Air Mad to Mandritsara on Saturdays. They had already booked in for their Air Mad flight when to their surprise the MAF plane landed for them! After persuading the Air Mad staff to release their luggage because they needed to return to Mandritsara straight away, they joined Mike, the MAF pilot. Anyway, to get to the point of my story, we have to refuel the MAF plane. This involves loading two 40 gallon drums of aviation fuel (one completely full) onto Johan's pick-up, which is no mean feat in itself. A full drum of fuel is extremely heavy, and rolling one up a plank is quite tricky. Then at the airstrip, the fuel has to be pumped by hand from the drum into the plane's wing tanks. In fact, we only need the partly-filled drum, so our efforts in getting the other drum into the pick-up are wasted! At least it is easier getting it off!

Annie decides that as MAF is flying from Mandritsara to Tana today and returning on Wednesday to collect us, that she will take the opportunity to visit Tana for a few days. In particular, she wants to arrange for her motorcycle insurance, as all the other documentation has arrived to enable her to ride it. It has been stored in one of the containers for the past two years, waiting for the bureaucracy to catch up.

We make sure the MAF plane takes off okay, watched by a considerable crowd of people, and return to the house for lunch of escalope of veal in a pepper sauce, with carrots, peas and rice.

In the evening we go for the last time to the Restaurant Belle Vue for steak and chips. Annie has asked Eddie, the Belgian working with the Catholic sisters on a water supply project, to take her place, so there are six of us. We fancy having *"banana flambe"* to follow the main course, but are told *"tsimiss"* (none) – which applies to every dessert on the menu! Some restaurant!

The evening is rounded off by watching the video *"Groundhog Day"*, the story of a man who is forced to re-live the same day until his life changes into something worthwhile. There is quite a spiritual message in that film, too.

Madame Radesena ironing the hospital curtains

Re-fuelling the MAF plane

Day 27: Sunday 17th November 1996

At the side of the church building, a plot of ground is being built on. Yesterday morning as we passed on our walk from the market we saw a gang of men hard at work, watched over by Monsieur Azad and his wife. This morning is similar, and they are wasting no time in getting the house built. It will contain eight rooms, each of which will be let for the sum of 100,000 *fmg* (£17) per month. There is a shortage of accommodation in Mandritsara, and Monsieur Azad is already one of the biggest property owners, as well as one of the most unpopular. His wife owns the building which was let to the Good News Clinic, overlooking the airstrip.

The interesting thing about their building work is the things they seem to have picked up from our work at the hospital – using reinforcing rods and string lines to mark out the line of the trenches, for example. When he sees me taking an interest in the work, it causes him great amusement as I realise he has "stolen" our ideas.

Church service is very long today, and the heat is sweltering, with very little breeze, and we are packed tightly on the back row. It starts just after 8.30am and does not finish until 11.00am, with communion to follow! The reason for this is not the preacher, Johan, who spoke for half an hour, but a party of Malagache from Scripture Union. Almost at the end of the service, they are asked to say a few words about why they are here. There are 12 to 15 people in their delegation, and four of them speak at length, introducing each other, for almost half an hour. Then, to cap it all, the pastor asks if the congregation has any questions. The question and answer session goes on for some time. It all takes place in Malagasy, of course, and by this time we have no interpreter.

We almost decide to leave the service before the end, but it is fortunate that we don't. We are paying little attention to what is happening when I hear my name as the pastor asks me to the front to speak to everyone. This is a real surprise, with no warning given, but he knows that this is our last Sunday as we will be leaving Mandritsara on Wednesday.

Since Dr Jeannine had been on duty at the hospital last Friday and so was unable to attend the dinner with everybody else, we have invited her to lunch today. We organise a barbecue with Johan, Beatrice and Doris. Julia, Jeannine's friend, spends most weekends with her, so we extend the invitation to her also.

Missionaries are always wary of the locals becoming dependent on them. The barbecue gives us an example of the boot being on the other foot! Johan has difficulty lighting the barbecue, so he asks Idoxy's husband Bienvenue to come and light it. All the locals cook with charcoal two or three times every day, so are very proficient at setting a good fire.

We want to use up meat from the freezer, so we barbecue chicken, steak and veal, and have a large selection of salad dishes. We follow this with fresh pineapple, pawpaw and lychees.

Jeannine expresses great surprise that the men cook the barbecue, and help to clear away and wash the dishes. In Madagascar, the culture is very different and the roles of men and women are clearly defined. Beatrice explains to her the Christian principle that whilst the man retains final authority in the family, the relationship is based on love, trust and respect, which leads to a mutual sharing of tasks.

Last night, Adrien was on duty at the hospital, and conducted a short service, including music with his guitar. The service was for the benefit of the two new mothers and their families, and the staff on duty. It was very much appreciated, particularly by the family who have just started coming to church, who commented that they had never had or heard anything like that before. People who have never heard the gospel before are amazingly open to the working of the Spirit, so unlike people in Britain whose hearts are hardened to the gospel.

Fresh fruit, pawpaw, pineapple, mango, banana, lychee

We learn over lunch that there is to be a second ballot in the Presidential election. The current President, Albert Zafy, has only received about 20 percent of the votes, whereas the former President, Didier Ratsiraka, has gained about 36 percent. The turnout is very high because voting is compulsory, but any candidate needs over 50 percent to win.

Ratsiraka is a retired admiral and a former Marxist who ruled Madagascar for 16 years before losing to Zafy in the last Presidential election in 1993, after political unrest and repression had paralysed the country for months. The current election is taking place because Parliament impeached Zafy for violating the Constitution and exceeding his powers.

Ratsiraka has campaigned on promises of establishing a *"humanistic and ecological republic"* in Madagascar, where most of the people live in chronic poverty. It would appear that whoever wins, there could be a time of political unrest and instability, and we need to pray that the work of AEF and other missionaries is not affected.

[Afternote: We learn in early January 1997 that the publication of the election results is suspended

after Zafy demands a recount of the second ballot. In a country of 14 million people eligible to vote, Ratsiraka is ahead by just 32,000 votes, and Zafy has made claims that the counting of votes has been rigged. The prospects do not look good.]

The afternoon gets hotter and hotter, and the air is very still with hardly any breeze, so unusual for here. As the sun begins to set, we decide to go for a walk to try to cool off – it is often cooler outside than in. Unfortunately, dusk is the worst time for mosquitoes, and I return with three unwelcome bites. We have been quite fortunate and generally have not been bothered with mosquitoes. We brought out with us an electric mosquito killer which we plug in the bedroom each night, and this keeps the room clear. Some of the doors and windows have mosquito screens, although they do not fit very well. We sleep with one window open (but screened) to keep us cooler. The first few nights we slept with a mosquito net over the bed, but we found it rather stifling and almost impossible to get out of bed in the middle of the night! So we have not used it since (naughty, naughty!) and don't seem to have suffered because of it. In the rainy season, though, we would have little choice but to use the net. We continue to take malaria tablets, some daily and others weekly, and will continue to take them for four weeks after we return. They are due to be finished just before Christmas, thank goodness.

～ • ～

Day 28: Monday 18th November 1996

The morning routine is always the same – wake for the first time between 5 and 5.30am, get out of bed at 6am. After washing, shaving, etc. I go round opening the living room outside doors to let the breeze in, opening living room windows and fitting the purpose-made mosquito screens, and taking the kitchen windows off its hinges and replacing it with its purpose-made mosquito screen. Gemma, the Mann's cat, is always anxiously waiting to come into the house, and loves to be given a bowl of milk and be fed on the odd scrap of toast.

Although there are gaps around all the screens, we don't seem to have been bothered with mosquitoes or insects in the house. Of course, later in the rainy season is the worst time for mosquitoes as they breed, and they are especially prevalent at the hospital. However, there has been plenty of geckos or small lizards, in the house. They do not bother us as we are used to them from our time living in the Caribbean, and they eat any insects or spiders that come into the house. They can be quite noisy though, as they make a loud clicking sound to each other from room to room. That can be a bit disturbing if you are just falling asleep. When we first arrived, it sounded like a bird, but not many birds make calling noises at night.

Idoxy is not feeling too well today as she has had her top front teeth out, so Sheila takes her some home-made soup that has been in the freezer. She is absolutely delighted – it takes so little to create happiness and gratefulness with an act of kindness. She goes to her cupboard and returns with a gift – a beautiful Bible holder made from colourful raffia, the same material that is used to weave mats, baskets and bags of all shapes and sizes.

Sheila has been clearing the cupboards and freezer ready to distribute what we have left over: some to the girls upstairs; some to Johan for his return in January; and to Idoxy and Gisele. A little later, Sheila explains to Idoxy and Madame Radesena, the *"maid"* or helper, that they can each have one of Sheila's dresses, and they carefully choose which one they want. They are highly delighted and chatter like excited schoolgirls, and eventually come to Sheila and ask if it is time to have their photos taken. Then they strip off to put the new dresses on, and insist that Sheila takes their photos.

Madame Radesena and Idoxy

Raffia Bible holder

Idoxy has also bought us some coffee beans from the market, which she then roasts for us to take back as gifts – she got four cups, about 2 lb in weight, which cost us 4,000 *fmg* (65p). In the afternoon there is a visit from the widow of the first President of Madagascar, who owns the house and property we are staying in. She wants to discuss the continued renting with Johan and to visit the hospital to see what has been done. Johan is able to use the opportunity to get permission for alterations to the property they want to carry out – firstly, the addition of the dining room upstairs for Beatrice and Annie, and secondly, adapting some of the outhouses for use as a guest house for future guests and short term workers. The idea is that this will be self-contained, consisting of a shower room and toilet, a dining area, a double bedroom, and eventually also a single bedroom. There is not much structural work to be done, but a lot of finishes and the addition of doors, sanitary ware, furniture and fittings etc. Neither project will commence until Johan returns next year, but each of the missionaries has contributed to the anticipated cost.

Sheila witnesses a very sad scene when a father carries a dead baby along the road from the Government hospital, followed by the mother, wailing and crying. It is a scene that preys on Sheila's mind all night. Mourning here is very open, with family, friends and neighbours sharing the experience and visiting the bereaved. It is suggested that this helps people to get over their grief quicker by enabling them to deal with it.

~ • ~

Day 29: Tuesday 19th November 1996

All too soon, the last day at work has arrived. It is a delayed start because firstly the Pastor has visited Johan at 7am to discuss things, knowing it is his last opportunity, and also Idoxy brings him gifts and letters to take back to his family.

Sheila and I have decided to give a love gift to HVM to be used to buy the bricks for the first part of Phase 2 to help the short term funding problems. The bricks that have been ordered should be enough for the laundry, the ward block and the new house for two families. So it is particularly pleasing that this morning Johan and I took Madame Azad to Alfonso, the brick supplier, as she is providing the transport for the bricks. I am able to see the bricks that our gift has been able to provide and take a photo.

Brick kilns for firing bricks

Rafia basket

Meanwhile, Sheila goes to the market for the last time, with Gisele and Doris. In particular, she wants to buy some *"voandalana"* or *"fruit of the road"* for Madame Vao. It is traditional to bring back some *"fruit"* from the area you have just visited for your host, so she takes her some local honey, which is bought and sold in old bottles. She also buys a small raffia basket used for winnowing rice.

On her return from the market, Sheila prepares a cardboard box loaded high with the left-over groceries and provisions for

Gisele, together with clothing and toiletries for both Gisele and Adrien. Gisele is ecstatic with the gifts, shooing the children out of the room as she realises there is chocolate for Christmas and an advent calendar for them. She has never seen an advent calendar before, and has to have it explained to her. Many of the gifts she will put away for Christmas, as a special treat.

We also decide to give a small monetary gift to Adrien and Gisele; Olivier and Ravo; Jeannine and Hanitra to give them each an extra treat for Christmas and to thank them for their kindness to us. It is a salutary lesson that we can bring such happiness to people at such a small cost to ourselves. When we consider their generosity and sacrificial giving, we realise how little we really know about sacrificial giving, giving that really costs something.

In the afternoon, both of us return to the hospital. I make my final checks on progress, give further instructions to Jean via Johan and say *"valoma"* to all the workforce, then pack up all my things, placing the survey instruments in the maintenance container for security.

As far as work progress is concerned, the Autoclave Building foundations are ready for the concrete ground slabs; the Laundry and Wash area foundations will be complete by the end of the week; the Ward Block concrete footings are 80% complete with the stone blocks about to start; and the House footings are being dug. Although we haven't completed all I had planned, looking back we have achieved a great deal, and I have every confidence that the workers will be able to finish off when we leave.

This evening we sign the official HVM visitors' book, and Beatrice also has a visitors' book that we also sign. Then it is the worst job of all – starting to pack.

CHAPTER ELEVEN
Preparing to Leave

Day 30: Wednesday 20th November 1996

On our very last morning in Mandritsara, we receive a caller at 6.30am whilst Sheila is still in bed. He is actually selling bread, the delicious baguettes that are available in Tana. If only he had visited before, we could have enjoyed fresh tasty bread regularly. Not that the bread Sheila baked was not good, of course, but the baguettes are particularly nice.

Jeannine calls to wish us *"bon voyage"* on her way to work as we finish our breakfast, and a few tears are shed. We set about completing the final packing, cleaning up the house, and giving away the remnants from the fridge and freezer, when we suddenly hear the sound of an aircraft. In Mandritsara this only occurs about twice a week, and today the only flight expected is the MAF plane to take us to Tana, due at 10.00am, but it is only 8.00! Everyone goes into sudden panic as the plane circles overhead, appearing to have the same blue stripes on its tailplane as the MAF colours. Beatrice and Doris are at the market, and rush back to see what is happening.

Meanwhile, Johan calls up MAF on the radio, and Emil reports that he doesn't think it is him, because he hasn't left Tana yet! Panic over. I finish packing and help Johan to pack away his computer and other valuable equipment into his container for security until he returns in January.

At about 9.30, Bea takes Johan's pick-up to meet the MAF plane, and comes back with Mike Frith (the pilot) and Annie, returned after her few days in Tana. She is glad to be back, but sorry her stay was so short and that she didn't achieve all she set out to do. That seems an accurate summary of life in Madagascar, particularly for us. While Mike refreshes himself with coffee and some of Sheila's delicious banana bread, we load the pick-up with all the luggage and are soon ready for departure.

Before we leave the house, a number of people call by to say their goodbyes. There are also quite a few at the airport, and Sheila is quite tearful. There are to be seven passengers on this return flight, which will help to reduce the cost our Church needs to pay. Apart from ourselves as the charterers, there is Johan, Beatrice and Doris, Adrien (who will be attending HVM business meetings in Tana), and the supplier of the *"boullion"* (granite stones) for Phase 2.

At the airstrip we have to go through the procedure of being weighed with all the luggage to ensure we do not overload the plane. Its capacity when Mike is the pilot is 820 kg, and the bathroom scales carried on the plane show a total of 740 kg, so all is well. We eventually take off for Tana at 10.40am, and I once again have the privilege of being seated in the front beside the pilot, with Sheila and Johan occupying the seats immediately behind.

After the flight with Emil Kundig when all communications with air traffic control were conducted in French, I am a little surprised that Mike uses English throughout. He explains that English is the international language for air traffic control, and for internal flights in Madagascar it is a matter of choice as to the use of English or French. He prefers to use his native tongue so that if there are any communication problems, the controller has them rather than him. Also, many of the Malagasy controllers like to practice their English, so it is good for them.

Immediately after take-off, Mike banks the plane steeply so that we can fly directly over the hospital to see the Phase 2 work. We can actually see them working, and manage to take a few photos. There is little cloud during the flight, but it is very hazy due to the air pollution caused by so many bush fires. During our last week in Mandritsara, the air pollution has gradually increased so that by three or four o'clock each afternoon it has been very smoky, often blocking out the surrounding hills and mountains altogether.

It is very distressing to see the damage caused by these fires, which are set deliberately by the local people. The result is deforestation, a complete loss of trees, shrubs and rainforest, which in turn causes severe soil erosion during the rainy season. The resultant heavy silts wash down into the rivers and lakes, killing the fish and plant life which are dependent on clean water. In addition, the natural habitats of much of Madagascar's unique animals, flora and fauna are destroyed. While efforts are being made to re-educate the people, the traditional ways of doing things continue to take precedence, as they cannot see the long term picture. We in the western world are not innocent bystanders in the ecological disasters throughout the world, either, before we start to think how much better we are!

Anyway, I think that's probably enough environmental concern for one day!

We land at Tana at 11.50, and by 1.00pm are at Madame Vao's guest house, having borrowed MAF's Nissan Vanette for our short stay in the capital. The charges are quite reasonable – 1,000 *fmg* (16p) per km including fuel. At least this means we can get out and about as we want, without having to rely on taxis. Dr Adrien is also staying with us at the guest house so that he is available for the meetings he and Johan are to attend, but Beatrice and Doris are staying with the Kundigs.

Adrien is to sleep in the main house, and this time Johan, Sheila and I are on the first floor of the guest accommodation. This is much nicer than below, with better finishes. The small guest block has an external stair at one end, leading to the front door which opens into a living room area with easy chairs and a coffee table. To the right is the shower and toilet, with an open kitchen off the living area. A slightly raised section leads to the dining area, behind which is a screened-off section with two single beds. At the very end, opposite the front door, is a door leading into a roomy double bedroom. It is very light and airy, and a delight to stay in.

After another of Chou Chou's delicious lunches, we set off for the zoo – Johan, Sheila and me. Being in Mandritsara for virtually all our stay in Madagascar, we were not able to visit any of the National Parks or rainforests, so we have seen little of the island's famous wildlife and have decided to visit Antananarivo Zoo. Non-residents are only charged 20,000 *fmg* (just over £3) per person. Most, if not all, of the animals here are endangered species or are of indeterminate numbers. The causes of so many becoming endangered with extinction include the fires and deforestation mentioned before, hunting for food, and catching for sale.

Within the zoo are many types of lemur; some crocodiles; Madagascar fish eagles (huge, impressive birds of prey); giant tortoises over 200 years old; snakes; lizards; frogs; birds; etc. It is set in a pleasant wooded area with wide open spaces and lots of water – not the traditional concrete and steel structures of many of the old European zoos. Many of the lemurs are uncaged, living on little islands separated from the main paths. Unfortunately, others are caged and some of these exhibit signs of stress – jumping up and down on the spot; running at the bars, repetitive actions, etc. – generally uncharacteristic behaviour.

The giant tortoises are incredible creatures. One is very close to the fence and is almost three feet in diameter, with a huge pendulous head that he seems to have great trouble in keeping in the air, and wrinkled leathery skin that betrays his extreme age. As we watch, he yawns in slow motion – opening his mouth very wide and keeping it open for many seconds, allowing Sheila time to photograph it. As she snaps it, another tortoise from quite a distance away comes trundling down the slope towards us, with the bandy, rolling gait that looks so ungainly but is characteristic of the tortoise.

The crocodiles look extremely nasty creatures, but do not stir. One is completely out of the water, one is half-in and half-out, and a third is completely submerged, with just his bulging eyes showing. Their apparent laziness belies their great speed and frenzy in attack – something to keep well clear of.

We take a cool fruit drink in the shade beside one of the lakes before returning to the main entrance where the National History Museum is located. This is just one large room, but contains the skeletons of many extinct animals, including dinosaurs found in Madagascar. There are also many stuffed animals and birds, and thousands of insects, moths and butterflies, all indigenous to Madagascar. Many of the latter exhibits are huge, and some are incredibly beautiful. It is a time to reflect on the beauty and variety of God's creation, contrasted with the sinfulness of man's destruction of it in so many different ways.

Before our return to the guest house, we decide to visit the Queen's Palace, as we are close to it. The original palace was a timber structure designed by a Frenchman, who used massive timbers in its construction. In the 1920's an Englishman built a stone structure around the older timber one, and it became a very impressive monument, standing proudly on the top of a hill for all to see. Just over a year ago, it was opened to the public but had very little security. Shortly afterwards it was deliberately set on fire, and all the inside was destroyed – including all the timberwork and the national treasures that were stored in the palace.

Antananarivo has only two ancient fire engines, and such were the crowds and vehicles trying to get up the steep hills and narrow roads to see the fire, that they took a considerable time to get there. When they did arrive, they found the water pressure was too low for their hoses, so were forced to watch impotently as the fire burned itself out. With a typical case of shutting the stable door after the horse has bolted, security at the Queen's Palace is now extremely tight, with about ten armed soldiers on duty at the gate. There is a strict rule about no photography, and in spite of Johan's fluent Malagasy, trying to convince the chief that all we want is a souvenir of Madagascar, he refuses on the basis that it is *"more than my job's worth"*! Such people are everywhere. We get the impression that for a small bribe, the rules could be bent a little, but we are not prepared to use such methods.

The view of Tana from that area is quite breathtaking, with a great view from above of the football stadium and new indoor stadium next to it. Unfortunately, by this time the light is bad and it is still very smoky, so we are unable to take any photographs.

It has been a very eventful day, and Sheila never travels well (like a bad wine?), so we retire to bed early.

~ • ~

Day 31: Thursday 21st November 1996

With shutters on the windows, it is much darker in the bedroom and we are able to sleep on a little in the morning, breakfasting at 7.45am with the much anticipated baguettes. MAF's Nissan Vanette that we are using will only start when warm, so we have to push-start it, out the drive and down the hill. It is very easy to get out of breath in the comparatively high altitude.

A Swiss couple, John and Sylvie, are also staying at Madame Vao's guest house. They are on an extended holiday, having already been to Chad and Cameroon before arriving in Madagascar a few days ago. They have their meals at the Kundigs' house, who are looking after a total of ten Swiss people at the moment. We take John and Sylvie to the Kundigs' to pick up Beatrice and Doris, so that all seven of us can visit the Craft Market. This has a bad reputation for thieves and pick-pockets, so we have to remain vigilant and wary at all times. Once we are in amongst the stalls themselves, which are all wooden huts, we are safe because the stall holders chase away any beggars or potential thieves, knowing they are bad for their business.

We are able to use our skills in bartering and haggling, but are very much spoilt for choice. The wide range of beautiful hand-embroidered tablecloths and blouses; carvings and other wooden goods, and crafts of all descriptions, makes choosing very difficult. There is much less pressure on buying than in the Zuma, and far fewer people. Sheila buys some blouses, a table runner and a wooden model of a rice pounder, like a mortar and pestle. Rice production is such a major part of life in Madagascar that it is portrayed in all its various stages, from preparing the ground to cooking and finally eating it.

Craft market in Tana   *Wooden model of rice pounder*

After lunch we return to the city centre for more shopping, this time in conventional shops. We want some T-shirts, more cards to use as Christmas cards, and a few more gifts to take back with us. We leave Johan and Adrien in a café discussing their forthcoming meeting with the European Community about the Contract for funds for Phase 2. On completion of our shopping we return for a cold drink and find they are still there, hard at it.

Their meeting with the E.C. goes well, although the Contract is still not quite ready for signing. However, they are able to resolve a number of outstanding difficulties and bring the signing a little closer. One of the main problems has been that there are ten projects due to receive E.C. money in Madagascar, and because one of them has gone over budget, a rescheduling of the funding has had to be done, and approval of this is awaited from Brussels. This will not affect HVM, apart from delaying execution of the Contract.

The other difficulty is with the Architects, MSAADA, who require payment in US dollars instead of Malagasy francs (*fmg*). The E.C. refuses to do this, as they want to encourage the local economy as much as possible, so Johan and Adrien need to meet MSAADA tomorrow to tell them payment must be in local currency. They leave their meeting positively, with no apparent insurmountable obstacles, but of course HVM first applied for a grant in 1993, so great patience and perseverance is still needed.

$$\sim \cdot \backsim$$

CHAPTER TWELVE
Homeward Bound

Day 32: Friday 22nd November 1996

It has finally come – our last day in Madagascar. It really does not seem that five weeks have elapsed since we first arrived, and yet so much has happened in that short time and most of our aims have been achieved. We plan to have a leisurely last day so that we can relax and get ourselves ready for the long flight home this evening. By now, we have had all the experiences we need, nothing more can happen, surely. Little do we know!

Sheila and I leave Madame Vao's after breakfast with her to hail a taxi to take us into the town centre, to the Zuma, the big Friday market. Although most of the taxi drivers can speak French, we have a piece of paper with us giving our address so that we can safely get back to the guest house on our return for lunch. We do not walk far before a taxi stops, we negotiate the price of 5,000 *fmg* (80p), and we climb aboard. Most of the taxis in Tana are over 20 year-old 2CV's, and this is no exception. However, it is possibly the worst one we have been in and is literally falling apart. The door handles inside are lengths of electrical cable, the windows are wedged in position (partly open), the windscreen is a mosaic of cracks, and the driver is dressed in rags! We do not get far before he pulls into a petrol station to fill up. Turning to me, he then asks for the fare money to pay for the petrol! During the rest of the journey, at every opportunity, he switches off the engine to save fuel, and coasts down the hills, ignoring the impatience of other motorists behind him. But we arrive safely, and have the satisfaction of helping him to earn some money that day.

Having experienced the Zuma when we first arrived, we know what to expect, and Sheila is looking forward to the haggling and getting what she wants. Fortunately it is not quite as crowded as the previous occasion so we feel less claustrophobic and explore the market for a much greater distance. Even then, we only see a fraction of what is reported to be the world's largest outdoor market.

Sheila wants to buy a shopping bag, made of colourful woven raffia, and has the advantage of knowing the going rate for such a bag from Beatrice. She sees one she likes and asks the price. Their reply of 100,000 *fmg* (£16) brings laughter from us to let them know what they are asking is much too high. After some haggling, they refuse to budge from 45,000 *fmg* and we have only offered 25,000 *fmg*. So we walk on to find more stalls selling the same bags.

Meanwhile, the original sellers follow us for a considerable distance, trying to persuade us to buy. At another stall, we stop and ask their price – 45,000 *fmg*. Sheila triumphantly turns to the first seller, telling him that this stall has started at 45,000, so his price is clearly too much! Each time the second stall holder lowers her price, the first matches it, until we are able to get the first bag, the colours Sheila wants, for 30,000 *fmg* (£4.80) as we intend. As the man leaves us, he grins and says *"tres difficile"* indicating the hard time we have given him in making the sale.

We carry on, buying as the mood takes us, on the whole little things that are fairly cheap. A beautiful hand-embroidered blouse, a silk picture, two leather belts, a bread basket, some spices, etc. For some we bargain hard, but for others, we hardly bother. Whilst a certain amount of haggling is expected and enjoyed, there is a responsibility on us not to exploit the situation. Most of the people in the market are totally dependent on how much they sell to live, and they may accept a price below an item's worth, simply to be able to buy a meal for that day. Seeing the amount of work that has gone into producing something can make you feel guilty about the small sum of money you have negotiated.

The spices we buy are contained in small plastic bags, connected together in a long line. We can smell the pungent aroma emanating from some of the spices, which include saffron, cardamom, cloves, paprika, peppers, pimento, coriander, ginger and aniseed. Madagascar is, of course, famous for its vanilla. It is the second most expensive spice in the world, and Madagascar provides 70 percent of the world's supply. The vanilla pods grow on an orchid plant and have to be carefully cured after picking. The best pods are about 6" long and look like thick dark leather shoelaces, but with a marvellous aroma. To produce vanilla extract, the pods are crushed, its flavour is extracted by solvent, preserved in alcohol, and aged.

Vanilla pods from Zuma

Our return to the guest house after a cold drink in a pavement cafe is uneventful, and we arrive back before Johan and Adrien. Johan had left at 7am to collect some embroidered tablecloths he had ordered and then went with Adrien to their meeting with MSAADA. They are due back at 11.00 to interview one of Madame Vao's nephews, Jimmy, as a supervisor for Phase 2 works. As usual, they are a little late. Part way through the interview, they ask me to join them to ask technical questions to ascertain Jimmy's construction knowledge. He is a very pleasant young man and has certainly had construction experience in certain aspects of the work.

Over lunch, Johan receives a telephone call from Annie, who is now temporarily alone in Mandritrsara. We learn that the young girl who has been ill and in a coma for so long has finally died, and the family wants to return with her to their home village for the funeral. The family have been preparing themselves for the worst, and the drawn-out agony is now over for all concerned, and they recognise that the girl is in a better place.

After lunch, while Johan and Adrien go to their meeting with the Baptist ministers, we take the opportunity to have a rest before the long journey ahead of us. I also pack the purchases we have made over the past few days.

Johan eventually returns, a little concerned because the van is overheating. Shortly afterwards Beatrice and Doris arrive and we load up the van with our luggage and begin our long drawn-out farewells to Vao and her family. We leave for the airport at 4.10pm, but after about ten minutes the engine stalls and will not restart. I get out to try to push-start the van but with no success. As we push the van to the side of the road, I notice oil leaking. It's soon clear that it is not going to restart and we will have to abandon it.

Our thoughts race. Will we get to the airport on time? What will happen if we miss our flight? The next flight to Paris is not for a few days, and our tickets are not transferable. I need to get back to work. I offer a quick prayer, and almost immediately a taxi pulls over and disgorges its passengers. Johan quickly approaches the driver and explains our predicament. His car is the standard Citroen 2CV that forms the vast majority of taxis, and is not big enough for three passengers and all our luggage. The driver immediately hails the next taxi that comes along, and when it stops, dispatches its passenger to allow us to use both taxis. As usual, they are both extremely old and decrepit, and we share our luggage between the two. Johan takes the first, while Sheila and I share the second, leaving Beatrice and Doris with the van until we can arrange for Emil to collect them.

Both taxi drivers clearly think that we are in danger of missing our flight, as they race at breakneck speed. By this time of the day, there is a great deal of traffic on the road, and they weave in and out, overtaking at every opportunity and every half-chance. Many times we nearly come to grief with the oncoming traffic, but the driver swings away at the last moment when a collision seems a certainty. Our driver appears as if he doesn't know the way to the airport, because he sticks to the bumper of the taxi in front as if his life depends on it. He tailgates with a gap of only two feet between the cars. I can honestly say that it is the most frightening and dangerous ride I have ever endured.

On the way, Johan stops to make a telephone call to Emil at a public phone box, which are very infrequent. Eventually, we arrive at the airport at 5pm, much relieved to be in one piece and still on time. Our taxis are surrounded by porters, all anxious to help us with the luggage. Johan organises a few of them and negotiates a tip. Firstly we have to pay the airport departure tax of approximately £30, which is only payable in hard currency. I ask for the small amount of change due back to be paid in French francs (coins), so that we can use them at Paris to telephone.

We then book in without difficulty, and proceed to passport control. Our baggage is carefully inspected by customs, to make sure we are not taking out of the country anything we shouldn't. Our departure tax receipt is checked, and we go through another customs inspection for our hand luggage. This is followed by a security check, and we are ready to wait for our flight in the departure lounge. We can see through the windows that our plane is waiting on the tarmac. Once again, it is an Airbus A320 in Air Madagascar colours, although it is an Air France flight.

We are again seated on the upper flight deck, this time in Row 7 with all three seats together. Unfortunately, across the aisle is an American lady who chatters incessantly to the man next to her in a loud voice, and we find it extremely distracting and wearing. After a meal, we sleep fitfully but a little better than we expect. I do not bother to watch the in-flight film, because it is *"Le Jaguar"*, a French film dubbed in English.

The flight is exhausting, seeming to be much longer than on the way out. We arrive at Charles de Gaulle airport in Paris on time, 7.55am Madagascar time, 5.55am Paris time. We transfer to our flight to Heathrow which leaves at 7.15am. When we clear immigration and customs, we find a small reception committee waiting for us. Philip and Rachel have got up early on this Saturday morning and have come with Avon Joyce to collect us. We hear a little of the news on the drive back, and share a few of the many experiences of the last few weeks.

Someone asks us *"When are you going back?"*, and whilst we have no plans, we would both jump at the chance to return. I am reminded of the messages on the cards we bought, that once you have been to Madagascar, you will want to return; and that a piece of your heart is left behind when you leave. What does the future have in store?

CHAPTER THIRTEEN
An Update: 1997 to 2021

After we returned home, we were in demand to speak and show slides about our experiences, firstly at Newbury Baptist Church and other local churches, and then in 1997-1999 in Bermuda, where we had temporarily relocated to for my work. We turned many of these opportunities into fund raising ventures, such as providing Malagasy meals, coffee mornings, cream teas, and selling copies of my book, etc. From May 1997 to September 2005, we were able to send over £9,300 to help the work of HVM in Mandritsara.

In 1998, AEF merged with another missionary organisation, SIM ("Serving in Mission"), but the AEF missionaries in Madagascar decided to continue to operate the hospital independently from SIM. This did not, of course, prevent SIM from sending their missionaries to support the work, as they still do. Clearly I maintained an active interest in the work, supporting it prayerfully and financially and raising funds as previously stated.

The Friends of Mandritsara Trust (FoMT) was subsequently formed to take care of HVM's interests in the UK, and to raise funds for the work, and I became a founding member. I was registered as a Trustee in January 2001, later becoming Company Secretary, and eventually retiring from the position and as a Trustee in December 2015.

The work of HVM has gone from strength to strength and has been wonderfully used by God. Some of the provisions have been truly miraculous and at all stages He has provided the necessary funding. I doubt that I would recognise the hospital were I to re-visit now, it has changed so much. There is a surgical block with two operating theatres, an administration building, a classroom for training; a Community Health Department and a Maternity Department, more staff accommodation, and huts built for the families of patients to stay and look after them while they are bedridden.

To give you an idea of the scope of the hospital today, the out-patients department sees 2,000 patients a month; in-patients are provided with 57 beds, medical, surgical and maternity; the operating theatre performs 1,400 operations a year and is the only one in a 200 km radius; and the eye department has its own operating room performing 450 cataract operations alone each year. One of the beauties of medical mission work is that those to whom the gospel is preached can see the authenticity and fruit of what is preached in the practical care they receive. They can observe love and kindness in action.

As well as the hospital, the mission work extends to The Good News School; The Voice of the Good News radio station, Community Health work and the Nursing and Midwifery Training School, all developed as Malagasy Christians and missionaries from overseas have worked together to bring the love of Christ and the message of His gospel to the people in the Mandritsara district.

The other main change in the last 25 years, of course, is in the personnel at the hospital. Johan Coutigny was tragically called home to the Lord in 1998, Madame Vao in December 2016, and Dr Adrien more recently. Annie and David and Jane Mann have retired, Beatrice returned to Switzerland; Olivier resigned. Still serving at the hospital (with their current positions in brackets) are Theophile (X-ray technician, Pharmacy and Sunday School teacher) and his wife Madame Vololoniony (Head Nurse for paramedical staff); Dr Hanitra (eye surgeon and Clinical Director); Dr Jeannine (in charge of the Nursing and Midwifery Training School); Pastor Julien and his wife Claire; and Sarindra (Head of the Maintenance Department) and his wife Claudia (Oasis Guest House Manager). Today the staff numbers working for HVM are many times what they were when this book was first written.

Sheila and I had hoped we would be able to return to Mandritsara after I had retired in 2012, but the Lord had other plans. We looked after Sheila's mum until she went to be with the Lord in March 2019, just four months shy of her 100th birthday, and Sheila passed into the presence of her Saviour in February 2020, having been unexpectedly diagnosed with an inoperable and untreatable brain tumour the previous November. It is thus extremely unlikely that I will return on my own, but you can never say never about the Lord's work and where He will lead.

In closing, I encourage you to visit HVM's website at **www.mandritsara.org.uk** to see for yourself what a great work that God is doing there, and any support you are able to give by prayer or financially would be much appreciated.

God bless you.

ABOUT THE AUTHOR

Brian Rawlings is a retired Chartered Civil Engineer, having spent a career building on three continents. The countries he has lived in and built on include the United Kingdom, St Kitts & Nevis, Madagascar and Bermuda. Some of the projects he has worked on range from St Kitts Deepwater Harbour, Jubilee Line Extension, The Waterfront Project Bermuda and Arsenal's Emirates Stadium.

Brian lives in Bournemouth in the UK, and can usually be found in his garden, down the beach or at his church.

Special thanks to:

Africa Evangelical Fellowship,
for all their help.

Newbury Baptist Church,
for their financial and prayer support.

Sir Robert McAlpine Ltd,
for donating survey instruments.

Family and friends,
for their generous donations.

All those who phoned or sent emails.

Sheila,
for typing the manuscript.

Philip,
for the design and layout,
and producing the end product.

And especially,
to the people of Madagascar
for their love and hospitality.

Lightning Source UK Ltd.
Milton Keynes UK
UKHW020626121121
393843UK00001B/42

9 789937 097598